CULTURES OF THE WORLD

JORDAN

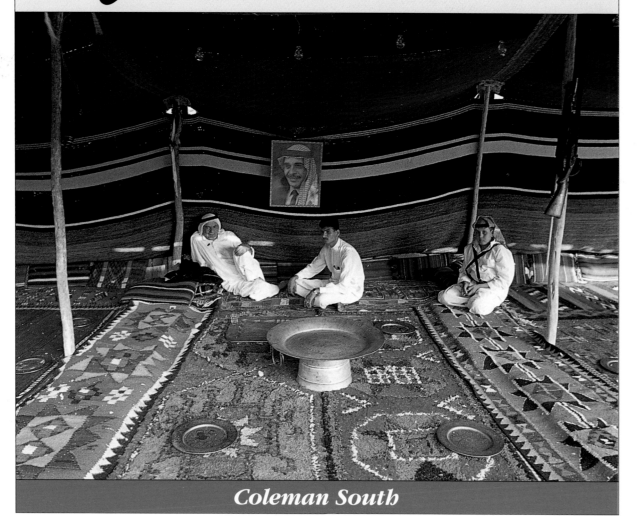

Coleman South

MARSHALL CAVENDISH
New York • London • Sydney

Reference Edition published 1997 by
Marshall Cavendish Corporation
99 White Plains Road
Tarrytown
New York 10591

© Times Editions Pte Ltd 1997

Originated and designed by
Times Books International, an imprint of
Times Editions Pte Ltd

Printed in Singapore

Library of Congress Cataloging-in-Publication Data:
South, Coleman, 1948–
    Jordan / Coleman South.
        p.   cm. — (Cultures of the world)
    Includes bibliographical references (p.   ) and index.
    Summary: Examines the geography, history, government,
economy, and culture of Jordan.
    ISBN 0-7614-0287-X (lib. bdg.)
    1. Jordan—Juvenile literature. [1. Jordan.]   I. Title.
II. Series.
    DS153.S57   1997
    956.95—dc20   96–18307
                                        CIP
                                        AC

INTRODUCTION

OF ALL THE ARAB COUNTRIES, Jordan is perhaps the most rural yet the most modern. It is also the most religiously and culturally homogeneous. The area east of the Jordan River has historically been part of Palestine, while the remainder of the harsh and mostly empty desert landscape has primarily been a land corridor as its Ottoman name, Transjordania, suggests. The Ottomans had used it as a route from Damascus in Syria to the holy Muslim cities of Medina and Mecca in Saudi Arabia. Before that, it was on the caravan route from Arabia to the Mediterranean. The British, who were the last outsiders to dominate the country, continued to use a modified form of the Ottoman name: Transjordan. The indigenous residents themselves have, until the last couple of generations, considered themselves citizens of Greater Syria, Iraq, or the Hejaz ("hee-JAZZ"), a provincial area of western Saudi Arabia, while the Palestinian population dreams of its own homeland. Of all the Arab countries, Jordan has had the closest relationship with its neighbor, Israel. It was the first country on the Arab peninsula to sign a peace treaty with Israel.

CONTENTS

Bedouin girl in Petra.

CONTENTS

Arab child in the Wadi Rum.

GEOGRAPHY

JORDAN BORDERS SAUDI ARABIA on the south and southeast, Israel on the west, Syria on the north, and Iraq on the northeast. It also has a few miles of land near the Red Sea. It covers 35,000 square miles (90,700 square km), making it about the size of Kentucky in the United States.

PHYSICAL FEATURES

There are three geographical areas, each with its own distinctive physical features.

THE JORDAN RIVER VALLEY This is the narrow, fertile valley alongside the Jordan River. It was here, about 10,000 years ago, that the inhabitants first started to plant crops and build villages, abandoning their nomadic lifestyle. Water-harnessing projects made agriculture possible and by 3000 B.C., crops were being exported to neighboring regions. During the early 1970s, new roads were built and irrigation projects, such as the ambitious King Abdullah (formerly East Ghor) Canal, were extended.

The area has hot, dry summers and short, mild winters—ideal conditions for cultivating crops. The average yearly rainfall is 12 inches (30 cm). The Jordan River Valley is situated along the country's western border with Israel and is part of the Great Rift Valley, the largest fault system on earth that runs 3,000 miles (4,830 km) from southwestern Syria to Mozambique in Africa. Unfortunately, the Jordan River Valley, considered the "food bowl" of Jordan, forms a meager 6% of the nation's land.

Above: **This lush spring is the largest of many found in the desertscape of the Wadi Rum.**

Opposite: **Bedouin man on a rock bridge, one of many natural sandstone and granite formations in the Wadi Rum.**

THE BLACK DESERT

One of the bleakest wastelands on earth exists in Jordan's northeastern desert. Composed mostly of vast fields of sharp, rough black lava rock, it is extraordinarily forbidding, unfit even for grazing sheep. This moonscape of volcanic mountains and smaller cinder cones extends into both Syria and Iraq and is the site of the ancient city of Jawa, the ruins of which can still be seen today. Bedouin superstition claims it is the land of the devil—*bilad ash shayton* ("bi-LAUD ash SHY-ton")—and they call it "the stony land of walking men"—in other words, fit only to pass through on the way to another place.

Since ancient times, the Bedouins have been able to use the poorest lands to their advantage. They camp for a few months at a time in one spot and graze their herd of goats, sheep, or camels. When the sparse fodder runs out, it is time to move on in search of new fodder. When grazing their herd, the Bedouins do not always respect the limitations set by national boundaries, and this has sometimes caused them trouble with government authorities.

THE DESERT The eastern and southern portions of Jordan are desert, with less than 2 inches (5 cm) of rain each year. It is mountainous and quite rugged in places (particularly in the south) and makes up 80% of Jordan's land. The northern area of the desert is volcanic rock, while the southern part is wind-eroded granite and sandstone. There are a few oases in the desert—fertile areas where springs provide water and crops can be grown. The Jordanian desert is part of the Syrian Desert—a vast, rocky territory that covers most of Syria, Jordan, Iraq, and a portion of northwestern Saudi Arabia.

WADI RUM ("WAH-dee ROOM") The desert in southern Jordan is full of hilly rock formations, and the area is called Wadi Rum. *Wadi* means "canyon" in Arabic, and the place is so named because the rugged hills make the flat land seem low, even though it is above sea level. Part of the movie, *Lawrence of Arabia,* was filmed here, and it was here that Abdullah, who later became king, organized the Bedouin troops that helped drive the Ottomans out of the country in 1918.

At one time sheep could be found grazing the once fertile canyon. Now, the land is inhabited only by a few Bedouins who live in goat-hair tents. Their subsistence depends mostly on tourists who are attracted by the spectacular scenery and go to hike, camp, and climb the rocks. The area is also the headquarters of the Desert Patrol Corps, or "camel" police. In an attempt to develop tourism, the government has, over the past several years, helped sponsor an annual hot air balloon event in Wadi Rum.

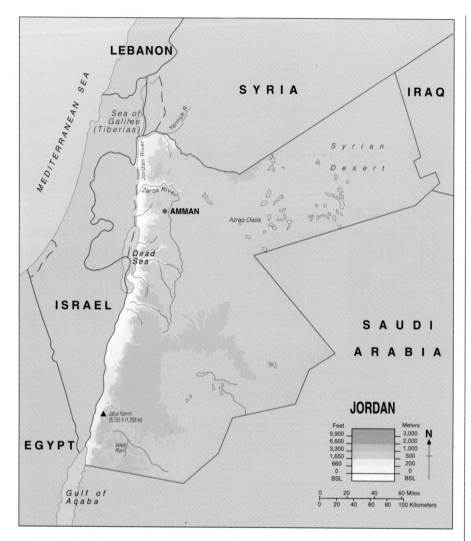

A wadi is a canyon in the desert where rainfall runs off the hills and soaks into the ground. The surrounding area can be cultivated when the farmer sinks a well to reach the water.

THE GREAT RIFT VALLEY

This giant crack was formed in the Pleistocene epoch (2.5 million years ago) when the African continental plate began to separate. It is still expanding at the rate of about 0.04 inches (1 millimeter) a year, slowly pushing the Arab peninsula away from Africa. The Jordan River Valley, the Dead Sea, the exotic, colorful cliffs of Petra, and the port of Aqaba are all in the northern part of the Great Rift Valley. Near its southern end is Lake Victoria in east-central Africa. The Dead Sea, near its northern end, is the lowest point on the earth's surface.

THE HIGHLANDS The narrow piece of land between the desert and the Jordan River Valley is a high plateau where the annual rainfall ranges from 13 inches (33 cm) in the north to 2 inches (5 cm) in the east and south. The climate here, like that of the Jordan River Valley, is Mediterranean, and many of the country's crops are grown here. Rainfall is unpredictable from year to year, and virtually all of it comes between November and May. Most years, before and after the rains, the country gets hot, dry winds from the Arab peninsula that sometimes create sandstorms.

At the turn of the century, Amman was little more than a village of 2,000 people. Its rapid growth began when it was declared capital of the newly independent nation of Transjordan in 1929.

MAJOR CITIES

Jordan's three largest cities—Amman, Zarqa, and Irbid—lie on the high plateau in the north. Ma'an lies farther south and Aqaba is near the Red Sea.

AMMAN The capital city is also the country's largest city. It is the site of the ancient Ammonite capital of Rabbath Ammon. A millennia later it became the Greco-Roman city of Philadelphia. By the 1800s it was a village of only a few hundred people when the refugee Circassians "refounded" it. The Circassians, who migrated to Jordan from the Caucasus region of Russia, established businesses and introduced large-wheeled carts and a system of dirt roads. However, it was only when Abdullah, Jordan's first king, set up government and built his first palace in Amman that the city's importance was established.

The city's major growth began in 1948 with a flood of refugees from the new state of Israel. Thousands more refugees arrived during the 1967

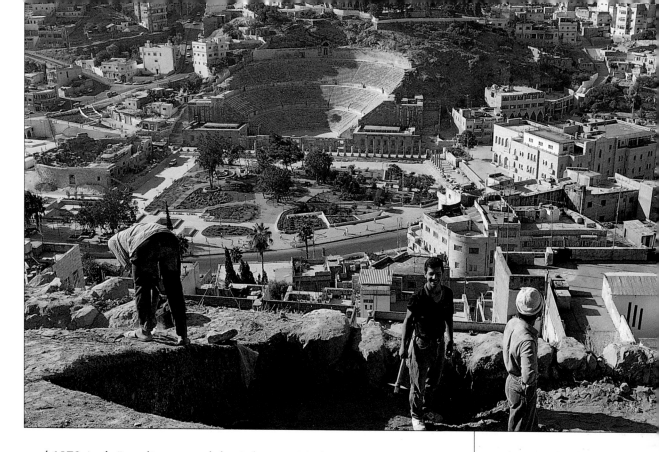

and 1973 Arab-Israeli wars and the Lebanese civil war. In 1991 Iraqis and Palestinians working in Kuwait and Iraq fled the Gulf War and found their way to Jordan.

Today, Amman is home to about two million people, or half of the country's population, and functions as the nation's financial and cultural center. It is a bustling city spread over seven hills called *jabal* ("JA-bul"), most of which are connected by wide boulevards. The city contains examples of beautiful Arabic-Mediterranean architecture, modern high-rise buildings, and many international businesses. Virtually all houses and other low structures are built from a light, honey-colored stone. Most of them have carved embellishment and wrought iron or stone balustrades.

There are two historical attractions in Amman. One, the ruins of a 6,000-seat Roman theater near the center of town, is still used for various events. The other attraction is the site of the Ammonite capital of Rabbath Ammon. There are also numerous ethnic restaurants, art galleries, and museums such as the Folklore Museum, the Museum of Popular Traditions, and the Archeological Museum.

The Roman theater was built in Amman in the 2nd century A.D., when the city was called Philadelphia.

11

Sunbathing in Aqaba with rugged mountains as a backdrop. The city in the background is Elat in Israel.

ZARQA This is Jordan's second-largest city with a population of about 400,000. It is a few miles north of Amman and has become a virtual suburb of the capital, acting as its industrial center. The city has an oil refinery and a tannery on its outskirts. Like Amman, it was established by the Circassians.

IRBID Located only a few miles from the border with Syria and Lebanon, this is Jordan's third-largest city with less than 200,000 people. Artifacts and graves in the area show that it has been inhabited since the Bronze Age. Today, it is the agricultural center of the country, located within a triangle formed by the Jordan, Zarqa, and Yarmuk rivers. Irbid is the site of the new Yarmuk University.

MA'AN Jordan's fourth-largest city is better known as the country's largest town. Located in the south near the end of the high plateau and the ruins of Petra, Ma'an is mainly a town of settled and semisettled Bedouins. It has little industry and no high-rise buildings.

AQABA The beauty of this place comes from its location near the Red Sea and a surrounding semicircle of craggy desert mountains. It is a hub of economic activity thanks to its large sea port, the only such port in Jordan. Fishing is carried out on a small scale. The area is modern and has facilities to cater to tourists who arrive in the summer. The beaches, blue water, and resorts along its short coast are a favorite of rich Arabs, as the place is only about 9 miles (15 km) from the Saudi Arabian border. New road and rail connections built in the late 1970s link it with Amman, giving Aqaba's economy a boost.

Irbid in winter, lying under a blanket of snow.

CLIMATE

The dry season is between April and October, while most of the rain falls during winter, from November to March. The average temperature varies from summer highs of about 100°F (38°C) in the Dead Sea area to winter lows of below freezing in the north. Aqaba, the Red Sea port, experiences warm year-round temperatures ranging from 60°F to 90°F (15°C to 32°C). The high plateau is cooler in the north, with temperatures ranging from below freezing to about 86°F (30°C). The Dead Sea valley is moderate in winter and very hot in summer, reaching 100°F (38°C). On the other hand, the desert suffers extreme temperatures—from below freezing in winter to above 100°F (38°C) in summer. The hottest temperature ever recorded in modern Jordan was in the Dead Sea area, reaching 124°F (51°C).

WATER

Jordan has only three significant sources of fresh water: the Zarqa, Yarmuk, and Jordan rivers, with the latter two shared by other nations. It borders the Red Sea through the Gulf of Aqaba. There is also the Dead Sea, the Azraq Oasis, and numerous small springs and seasonal oases.

During certain periods of the year, the Azraq Oasis attracts children to its cool waters.

RIVERS The Jordan River rises from springs on the southwestern slopes of Mt. Hermon (located on the boundary between Lebanon, Israel, and southwest Syria), 6,560 feet (2,000 m) above sea level. It has five separate tributaries on its course: the Dan, Hasbani, Banias, Zarqa, and Yarmuk. The first three originate and join the Jordan River in Israel near Lake Tiberias (the Biblical Sea of Galilee).

The Yarmuk is the major tributary and forms the border between Jordan and Syria for 25 miles (40 km), then the border between Jordan and Israel for a few miles before flowing into the Jordan River. After this confluence, the Jordan River runs 68 miles (110 km), creating the border with Israel for 25 miles (40 km) before flowing entirely into Jordan, into a deep gorge called Zor (part of the Great Rift Valley). It empties into the Dead Sea.

There are several small dams along this river system. One proposed dam on the Yarmuk has been delayed for nearly a decade because of disputes among Syria, Jordan, and Israel over the distribution of water. Jordan uses a substantial amount of water from both the Yarmuk and Zarqa rivers to irrigate its highland crops. Jordan and Israel together use 100% of their total water resources, so regular water shortages are common. In a land that is so arid, access to water is not just politics, but pure survival.

OASIS In eastern Jordan lies the extensive Azraq Oasis, the only permanent body of water in 46,000 square miles (120,000 square km) of desert. It provides refuge and water for thousands of animals.

THE DEAD SEA

Imagine water so dense that you cannot sink in it. That is the Dead Sea, a large inland sea so named by the Greeks who noticed that the salt water in it was so concentrated that it could not support life. There is no outlet to the sea and even though the Jordan River and small streams and springs feed it, an annual evaporation rate of 80 inches (203 cm) keeps the Dead Sea high in salinity. The water is seven times saltier than that of the oceans. It contains the following salts: chlorine, bromide, sodium, sulfate, potassium, calcium, magnesium, carbonate, and silicate. These minerals form bizarre shapes that protrude from the water in some places.

The sea is 46 miles (74 km) long and about 10 miles (16 km) wide. The surface of the water is 1,312 feet (400 m) below sea level, making it the lowest body of water on earth. Prior to 15,000 B.C. this was a lake 200 miles (322 km) long. But around that time the climate of the area became dryer and hotter, and the lake began to shrink, becoming ever saltier.

The Biblical cities of Sodom and Gomorrah are thought to lie under the sea's southern waters, submerged by a catastrophic earthquake in the time of the Hebrew prophet Abraham. The Israelis call it the Salt Sea, while the Arabs call it the Sea of Lot—so named for the Biblical story of the destruction of Sodom and Gomorrah when Lot's wife turned to look longingly at the home she was fleeing and was transformed into a pillar of salt.

Salt-encrusted rocks in the Dead Sea are caused by a high evaporation rate of the concentrated salt water.

FLORA AND FAUNA

Despite its being mostly desert, Jordan supports a significant amount of wildlife. There is also a growing amount of forest land as a result of the government's forestation policy.

Purple irises bloom from February to May.

WILDLIFE Most wildlife lives in the Shaumari and Azraq wetlands, wildlife reserves watered by the Azraq Oasis. Animals found there include the Arabian oryx, gazelle, ostrich, hyena, mongoose, ibex (a wild goat), sand adder (a poisonous snake), and more than 300 bird species including the white pelican, flamingo, crane, 15 species of duck, and seven of egret. Other birds found are the golden eagle, vulture, dove, and falcon. Many snakes, scorpions, and lizards thrive in the desert.

SEA LIFE At its northern end, the Red Sea divides into the shallow Gulf of Suez in the northwest and the mile-deep Gulf of Aqaba in the northeast. The Gulf of Aqaba has magnificent coral gardens inhabited by thousands of species of marine life, some of them unique to the area. Unfortunately, some of the coral and marine life have been dying in recent years as a result of pollution, overfishing, and heavy sea traffic to the Jordanian port of Aqaba and the Israeli port of Elat nearby.

A REAL UNICORN?

It is believed by some that the mythical unicorn was modeled after the Arabian oryx, even though the latter has two straight, sharp horns. The oryx has a striking appearance and the Arabs cherish it for its beautiful dark eyes. Its Arabic name—*maha* ("MAH-hah"), a common name for females—means "crystal" and is inspired by the pure white fur of its body. Evolution has given the creature a characteristic that also belongs to camels—that of being able to live for extended periods in intense heat with no food or water. This makes both animals ideally suited to life in the desert. Unfortunately, as with many creatures that have adapted to harsh environments, the oryx has fallen prey to hunters; many were killed in their natural habitat by the middle of the 20th century.

The Arabian Oryx World Herd Trustees was established in 1962 to restore oryxes to the wild, using zoo stock from around the world. Fourteen oryxes were shipped from Oman, Germany, Switzerland, Saudi Arabia, Qatar, and the United States to three special American zoos for breeding. When the Shaumari Reserve was completed in 1983, four male and four female oryxes were shipped from the U.S. zoos to Jordan. They have multiplied and are on their way to becoming a viable wild population again.

PLANT LIFE Jordan has about 35,000 acres (14,000 hectares) of forest, mostly consisting of evergreen oak, pine, and olive trees. Many olive trees grow wild as they have for thousands of years. The government began a reforestation program in 1948. Some thorny plants as well as palm trees grow in the desert, particularly in *wadis* and oases. The most common flowers are poppies, roses, irises, and wild cyclamen.

HISTORY

UNTIL THE EARLY 20TH CENTURY Jordan was thought of as part of Greater Syria, an ancient land comprising what is now Syria, Lebanon, Jordan, and part of Turkey in the northwestern corner of the Arab peninsula. Its history is part of an illustrious era going back 10,000 years. Greater Syria—or the Levant, as it is now called—is often referred to as the cradle of Western civilization and the crossroads of civilizations.

ANCIENT HISTORY

Jordan was historically the eastern part of what used to be Palestine. Its strategic site in the Middle East ensured that all the great early civilizations passed through the area; its history has been shaped by the Egyptians, Assyrians, Babylonians, Hittites, Greeks, and Romans. The land was fought over by these ancient peoples and contains some of the oldest known sites of civilization.

Around the 13th century B.C., there was an invasion of "peoples from the sea," believed to be the Philistines. They settled on the coastal plain of what was then Canaan in an area that came to be known as the Plain of Philistia—from which the name Palestine is derived. By the late 11th century B.C., however, the Philistines found themselves threatened by the exodus of Israelites from Egypt, led by the prophet Moses. Since then, the area's history has largely been that of invasion and conquest.

EARLIEST SETTLERS The early settlers were nomadic hunter-gatherers. Flints have been found in the Black Desert dating from the Stone Age, and

Above: **Ancient rock carving found in the Wadi Rum, indicating the presence of animals such as the horse and dog in prehistoric times.**

Opposite: **Colored sandstone rock in Petra, which means "rock" in Greek.**

Water chamber in Petra.

prehistoric drawings of cows and bulls have been discovered in the desert and Jordan River Valley. The Jordan River Valley is the location of crude settlements that originated around 8000 B.C., and there is evidence that the world's first wheat was cultivated in this fertile area.

A city known to archeologists as Jawa is the earliest known advanced settlement in Jordan, dating back to the Middle Bronze Age (circa 4000 B.C.). This was a massive stone city built in the Black Desert by a people of unknown origin who lived there for about one generation. It is believed that they moved westward, since later settlements in the Jordan River Valley and throughout Palestine show the same water technology and building methods.

There are two main theories concerning the people and their origins. One is that they moved from another urban culture in the east or north; the other is that they were local nomads who "invented" settled life. The first theory is considered the more likely. It is possible that they arrived in the spring when runoff from the snow and rain in the nearby mountains looked promising as there is usually no water in the summer.

JAWA—LOST CITY OF THE BLACK DESERT

Jawa must have been an impressive sight for anyone traversing the surrounding desolate landscape. The city covered about 30 acres (12 hectares)—most of it on a rise—in a *wadi*. A traveler approaching the city would have noticed its extensive planning. Outside the metropolis was a complex system of dams and canals, fed by winter runoff from the nearby mountains. The outer city walls were made of unworked stone set in rough courses with massive stone gates on stone hinges.

Inside the gates were flat-roofed huts with pounded mud floors, stone foundations, plastered walls, and wooden timbers supporting roofs of wooden slabs covered with mud-plastered reeds. The huts had stone benches along the interior walls, small pits in the floors, a hearth or two, and at least one round stone-lined storage bin—but no windows. (This is a desert with sweltering summer and freezing winter temperatures, and glass production was several millennia away.) Those who entered the massive, pentagon-shaped citadel first passed through another wall 20 feet (6 m) high and 13 to 16 feet (4 to 5 m) thick at the base. The houses here were larger than those outside and each outbuilding of the citadel was divided into 24 cells with three traverse corridors. The conclusion that can be drawn is that the inner confines of the citadel must have been dwellings built for the elite.

One can only guess what other things the visitor might have seen. Today, 6,000 years later, some sections of the inner wall still stand 20 feet (6 m) above the surrounding rock, and the cantilevered basalt slabs that held the roof are still in place. This amazing architectural technology was contemporary with such feats as Stonehenge in England and the pyramids in Egypt. Today, Bedouins still use parts of the ancient water collection and storage system to water their camels and sheep.

OTHER EARLY PEOPLES After the mysterious rise and fall of Jawa, many groups occupied the area: Amorites, Canaanites, Hebrews, Ammonites, Moabites, Edomites, and Arameans. The Ammonites formed a capital city, called Rabbath Ammon, where Amman now stands. All these peoples were Semitic tribes of nomads, many of whom were at constant war with each other over water usage and the question of whose god was the "real" one. The warring reached a height during the latter half of the 2nd millennium B.C. King David of the Hebrews, for example, attacked the Moabites and Edomites, killing two-thirds of all Moabites and the entire male population of Edom. The northern part of the area was conquered by outsiders: the Assyrians around 900 B.C., the Babylonians under King Nebuchadnezzar, then the Persians. The Egyptians, too, controlled the area for a time.

Roman triumphal arch built in Jerash in A.D. 129.

NABATEANS Even when the Assyrians and other conquerors came, they controlled only the northern part of the land that is now Jordan. The Nabateans ruled southern Jordan, part of the northwestern Arab peninsula, and Palestine for about 1,000 years, until they were defeated by the Roman general Trajan in A.D. 106. The Nabateans are often described as a people of Arab origin. They were primarily spice merchants who plied their trade along the "spice trail" from the Far East, dealing with Persians, Hebrews, Ptolemeans, and Selucideans (the later two were early Greeks).

Their successes can be attributed, as with the Jawaites, to their water technology in an arid climate. They developed an extensive system of large cisterns built to collect rainwater and snow melt, making the desert habitable. The cisterns were huge, square caves more than 100 feet (30 m) on a side. The openings were small and covered, marked with signs known only to the Nabateans.

THE ROMANS The Romans ruled this land as part of their Byzantine empire for several hundred years and left numerous remains. Jerash (north of Amman), for example, is sometimes called the Pompeii of the East and is one of the best preserved Roman sites in Asia. The Romans brought commercial success and innovation to the area, but as their rule began to disintegrate, the chaos of tribal warfare again took hold, and it was during this chaos that the most powerful force in the history of the Middle East—Islam—swept in.

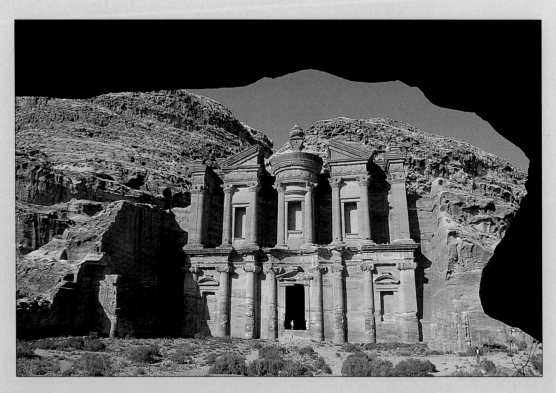

PETRA, THE ROSE-COLORED CITY

The pinnacle of Nabatean civilization, from about the 4th century B.C. to the 2nd century A.D., is still visible today in the ancient city of Petra. With an ample supply of fresh spring water, the city became a major stopping point on the caravan route from Arabia to the Mediterranean.

Petra is a city of elaborate facades in unique Nabatean and Greco-Roman architectural styles. They were carved into sandstone cliffs hundreds of feet high in a network of canyons that are part of the Great Rift Valley. Behind the often enormous facades are relatively small, square rooms. The hues of the cliffs are predominantly reddish-purple, and thus the city has become known as the rose-colored city. It was ideal for protection from enemies, since the main entrance was through the *Siq* ("SEEK"), a narrow, winding cleft in the sandstone. Its high elevation of 2,700 feet (820 m) above sea level and its location in the bottom of the gorges made it a cool place to live in the summer. In the winter, it sometimes snows on the heights while there is no snow at the bottom of the canyons.

During the Arab uprising against the Ottoman Turks in World War I, Petra was the site of a famous battle in which Lawrence of Arabia fought. Today, some Bedouins who service tourists live in the caves.

MIDDLE HISTORY

The soul of modern Jordan was formed during the century or so of Arab rule when Arabic became the common language and Islam the dominant religion. However, many Christians and Jews still remained in the area.

THE OMAYYADS After the death of the Prophet Mohammed in A.D. 632, his followers continued to spread his teachings. In the middle of the 8th century, the Omayyads, the strongest of the clans from the Hejaz, overran Greater Syria and established their headquarters in Busra ("BOOS-ra"), just north of what is now the Jordanian-Syrian border. From there, they conquered and ruled the entire Arab peninsula, northern Africa, and southern Europe—an area about the size of the former Roman empire.

Although the area that is now Jordan was not of great importance in the Arab empire, the Arab rulers built magnificent palaces and hunting lodges there and their ruins remain today. The Arab empire lasted for only about 100 years, but its linguistic, cultural, and religious legacy lives on today, more than 1,000 years later. As Arab rule declined, tribes and clans once again ruled their own small pieces of land in what is now Jordan.

Unlike the territory that is now Syria, where the Omayyads established a continuing tradition of urban life, the area of Jordan remained rural and nomadic.

THE OTTOMANS In the mid-16th century, the Ottoman Turks took over the Levant and the Arab peninsula. As with the previous empire, Jordanian land was not very important to the Ottomans except as a passage from the northern area to the holy cities of Mecca and Medina. The Ottomans named it "Transjordan," indicating its primary use as a land corridor.

They were strict overlords who imposed taxes and adopted a military style of government. However, they allowed local administration of the territory by Arabs loyal to them. As a result, there was a lack of social and economic development. Although there was order in the cities, the outlying areas were plagued by lawlessness. The Ottomans ruled for about 400 years until the end of World War I, when they were driven out of Arab lands in large part by the Bedouins living in Jordan and the Hejaz, backed by the British. Abdullah ibn Hussein, the man who later was to become king of Jordan and grandfather of today's King Hussein, led troops that were responsible for the first major Arab victory over the Ottomans.

20TH CENTURY

In order to understand the conflicts in this area, it is important to know a little about their causes. After the Turks were driven out, France and Britain—the winning European powers of World War I—bargained with each other to take over the land of the Levant for political, religious, and economic reasons. This self-interest combined with ignorance of the cultures involved led to the division of Greater Syria into what were to become the countries of Syria, Lebanon, Jordan, and Israel.

The most important development introduced by the Ottoman Turks was the Hejaz Railway. Trains could travel from Istanbul in Turkey to Aleppo and Damascus in Syria, and on to Amman. The railway line ended in Medina in Saudi Arabia.

Abdullah ibn Hussein meeting British Foreign Minister Bevin. He had the support of the British from the time he sought to drive out the Ottoman rulers through the time that Transjordan was established, and when Jordan gained its independence. His dependence on Britain often placed him at odds with other Arab rulers.

IN LIMBO The new League of Nations approved this partitioning of Greater Syria in 1923. Long before that approval, however, France had taken over what is now Syria and Lebanon, while Britain had taken over Palestine and Transjordan—the land that is now Jordan.

The principle of the League of Nations mandate was that Britain would help develop the area commercially and politically. Britain also had various self-interests in the area. These were to: 1) safeguard its route to India via the Suez Canal, 2) maintain access to a cheap source of oil from what is now Iraq, 3) maintain its power in the Mediterranean, 4) expand its commercial and financial interests, and 5) create a homeland for European Jews in Palestine.

The British sent political officers to three Jordanian communities to give several assurances. One was for political assistance in organizing the local government; another was that Transjordan would not be annexed to Palestine; a third, that Britain would not conscript residents for military service nor disarm them. Because of these assurances, Arab nationalists were at first in favor of the British presence and regarded it as protection from the French military forces in the north.

THE FIRST LEADER Abdullah ibn Hussein was born in Mecca in 1882 to a father who was a *sharif* ("SHAH-rif"), an Arab noble descended from the Prophet Mohammed. He spent part of his childhood and young adulthood in Istanbul, where his father was a ranking Arab in the Ottoman administration.

Abdullah and his brother Faisal had great dreams, but Abdullah's were perhaps the more grandiose: he wished to rule all the land that is now Syria, Jordan, Iraq, and northwestern Saudi Arabia (the Hejaz). His dream to rule Syria remained until his death. The British actually considered him king of Iraq for a short time to protect their commercial interests there. However, when the French drove Faisal, who had been crowned king of Syria, out of Damascus, the British "gave" him the throne in Iraq, thus firming up their interests in the region with two apparently loyal leaders. The two brothers, however, had used the British against the Ottomans and later maintained the alliance for their own protection as well as financial and other support.

Winston Churchill, Britain's foreign minister at the time, liked Abdullah from the beginning and convinced him to move to Amman from Ma'an in southern Jordan, where the future king had based himself while hoping to take over the Hejaz. Abdullah agreed to Churchill's request and set up his first headquarters in the home of a prominent Circassian.

TRANSJORDAN IN ABDULLAH'S TIME

In 1921 Transjordan's population was only 231,000 and there was no place that resembled a city; Amman at that time had only 5,000 people, the core of which were Circassian and Chechen settlers. The rest of Transjordan had the most ethnically and religiously homogeneous population of the Levant-Iraq area, with virtually everyone being identified by Arab clan, family, and tribal affiliation.

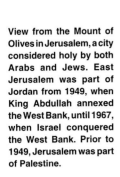

View from the Mount of Olives in Jerusalem, a city considered holy by both Arabs and Jews. East Jerusalem was part of Jordan from 1949, when King Abdullah annexed the West Bank, until 1967, when Israel conquered the West Bank. Prior to 1949, Jerusalem was part of Palestine.

THE BEGINNINGS Under British control, Transjordan became a state in April 1921. In October 1922, Abdullah went to London where he and British officials created the borders of the new nation, and he was officially made emir, or ruler, in late 1923. Britain pushed for a constitutional monarchy with an elected legislature, but Abdullah balked for the time being.

Abdullah was a nomad at heart, and despite the construction of his first palace in the mid-1920s, he still camped in his goat-hair tent for weeks at a time, moving throughout the country to build rapport with the Bedouins and win their loyalty. This started a tradition that King Hussein has continued to this day and that has established Bedouin loyalty to the crown. The country's first army was almost completely composed of Bedouins, and even today, the majority of those serving in the army are Bedouins.

ZIONISTS, REFUGEES, AND TURMOIL Britain's Balfour Declaration of 1917 (which became part of the League of Nation's mandate) guaranteed the Jews a homeland in Palestine if they wished to move there. This caused immense turmoil in Palestine and the surrounding area as militant Zionists began to arrive. Their stated goal was to take over all the land they considered holy to Judaism. The Palestinian people, who had lived there for more than 1,000 years, rebelled against the unwelcome settlers, and terrorist attacks soon escalated on both sides. The ensuing conflicts pushed some Palestinians into Transjordan, but the worst was yet to come.

The first serious rebellion against the League's mandates occurred in the mid-1920s in Syria, and the brutal French reaction drove many Arab nationalists into Transjordan, as did the civil war then raging in the Hejaz. Then, after a devastating earthquake hit Amman in 1927, the Jews in Palestine helped to rebuild the city.

Abdullah saw an opportunity for himself in this Jewish interest and offered to support the development of a Jewish homeland if the World Zionist Organization would use its influence to help him become king of a combined Transjordan-Palestine. This resulted in Jews actually purchasing land from Transjordan landowners and becoming settlers in the country.

With this historical backdrop, a formal Transjordan-Anglo agreement in 1928 resulted in a constitution that was unsatisfactory to most local residents, causing various demonstrations. Once calm returned, however, life went on without major upheaval for the next 20 years until after World War II.

ZIONISM

In 1878, Jews bought farmland in what was then Palestine. Their aim was to set up a community. At that time, there was much persecution of the Jews in eastern Europe. In 1897, Theodor Herzl created the World Zionist Organization. Waves of immigrants entered Palestine and set up agricultural settlements throughout the country. During World War I, British Foreign Secretary Arthur James Balfour declared that his government favored "the establishment in Palestine of a national home for the Jewish people." This led to the promise of British assistance embodied in the Balfour Declaration.

WAR AND INCREASED INDEPENDENCE In February 1946 Abdullah went to London to negotiate independence. Within a month a treaty was signed, but the weak, new country was still heavily dependent on British military and financial support. In March 1946 a constitution that gave almost complete power to Abdullah was passed, and on May 25 his lifelong dream was realized when he crowned himself king. The revised constitution also gave the country its modern name: Jordan.

Many events took place in 1948. Early in 1948 the Transjordan-Anglo treaty was revised, giving Jordan greater independence. In May, the nation of Israel was formed in Palestine (although native Palestinians outnumbered Jews two to one), and the armies of the Arab League, of which Jordan was a member, attacked Israel, resulting in the first Arab-Israeli war. As a result of these two events, hundreds of Palestinian villagers were killed and many others expelled. The exodus flooded Jordan with homeless Palestinians. The armistice at the end of the 1948 war divided the West Bank (the land west of the Jordan River) between Israel and Jordan, and gave Jordan the job of policing the border between the Israeli and Jordanian sections.

Truce period at the end of the 1948 Arab-Israeli war.

EAST BANK AND WEST BANK

Historically these terms were used simply to mean the parts of Palestine east and west of the Jordan River. Now the East Bank is sometimes used to mean Jordan itself, but only the area directly east of the river up to Amman.

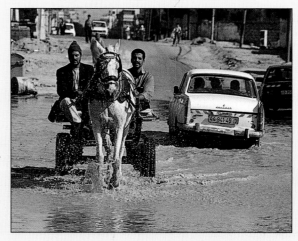

Politically, the West Bank is a bubble-shaped area—about a quarter the size of the original (pre-1967) Israel—that projects into Israel. This area is always marked on maps of Jordan and Israel. It includes cities of great historical importance to Muslims, Christians, and Jews—Jerusalem, Jericho, and Bethlehem, for example. When the land of Palestine was "given" to the Zionists by the Allies after World War II, the West Bank and Gaza Strip (then a part of Egypt) were excluded as zones for the Palestinians. In 1949 King Abdullah annexed the West Bank as part of Jordan, stirring up anti-government sentiment among the Palestinians.

In December 1949 Abdullah effectively annexed the non-Israeli part of the West Bank, setting up parliamentary elections (the first in the new country) to give credence to his annexation. The new parliament approved the land grab, but that was its only action, as Abdullah dissolved the body soon after. The Palestinians of the West Bank acquiesced for lack of a better alternative, but the king was assassinated in Jerusalem in July 1951. His grandson and the current king of Jordan, Hussein, was with him at the time and was hit by a bullet. A chest medal he was wearing stopped the bullet, miraculously saving his life.

In 1950 the population of Jordan's East Bank was only 476,000, while there were nearly a million Palestinians in the West Bank that was now part of Jordan. After Abdullah's death, with no appointed or apparent successor, Jordan's political leaders were paralyzed. Some wanted to form a union with Iraq, a few wanted Abdullah's son Talal to be crowned, while many others wanted Talal (who had both mental and physical disabilities) to step aside and allow his underaged son, Hussein, to be crowned.

A SHORT-TERM KING While the political battles raged, Talal was incommunicado in a Swiss sanitarium. When his doctors there gave him a clean bill of health in August 1951, he returned to Amman, where his half-brother Nayif was planning a coup. Knowledge of the coup reached the government, security was tightened, and the coup failed. Talal refused to step aside and allow his son to be crowned, so his coronation took place on September 6, 1951. However, he became increasingly violent toward his wife and children.

Before long the deterioration in his health became so obvious that the country's cabinet decided to seek his hospitalization. About this time Talal took a trip to the United States, and a "throne council" was formed in Amman. Jordan's prime minister at the time was a strong leader who convinced Talal to return to Jordan for hospitalization, leaving the throne council in charge until Hussein came of age. Then in August 1952, parliament voted to depose the sick king and crown the young Hussein. In September Talal went to Egypt for treatment before moving to Istanbul where he spent the rest of his life. He died in 1972.

A THIRD KING In December 1952 a new, more democratic constitution was installed, and in May 1953, Hussein was crowned. The young king, who had been educated at Harrow in Britain, was only 16 years old. The new king's mother, Zayn, was a strong woman, powerful behind the scenes, and had helped in ousting her incapacitated husband and getting her son crowned. She continued to exercise much influence in Jordanian affairs.

The first few years of King Hussein's rule were rocky. There were constant low-level border wars between Jordan and Israel, and he had problems with power-hungry prime ministers. Also, he was vehemently anticommunist and wanted to join the anticommunist pact along with Turkey and Iraq, but the populace wanted a socialist government, such as Egypt's or Syria's, and was violently opposed to this. The king gave in to the opposition but dissolved parliament with hopes of setting up one more compliant to his wishes. However, rioting, strikes, and overwhelming opposition to the parliamentary dissolution caused the king to reverse his decision. These things brought the country close to collapse—Saudi troops amassed near the southern border, curfews and martial law were imposed, and Britain prepared to send in paratroopers to support the Jordanian government. Britain's aid to Jordan lasted until the Egyptian takeover of the Suez Canal in 1957, after which King Hussein appealed for and won support from the United States. Thereafter, his leadership position was consolidated, although far from trouble-free.

JORDAN JOINS THE UNITED NATIONS

In 1954 parliament and all political parties were dissolved, and the government again imposed martial law, beginning a reign of terror that led to press censorship, mass arrests, and imprisonment and torture of perceived political opponents.

Jordan joined the United Nations in 1955. With Palestinians forming two-thirds of the population, tensions continued over political issues. The king expelled the British commander of the Arab Legion (the predecessor of the Jordanian Arab Army) and worked to strengthen his bond with other Arab leaders.

STRIVING FOR IDENTITY In early 1958 Syria and Egypt united to form the United Arab Republic. They were socialist countries friendly toward the Soviet Union and its allies. Because of King Hussein's strong anticommunist leanings, he was considered an enemy of both countries, and Syria closed its border with Jordan. At the same time, Iraq and Jordan united to become the Arab Federation, but this did not last—a socialist revolution in Iraq in July of the same year quickly ended the union.

At the time of the Iraqi revolution and again two years later, assassination plots were uncovered against King Hussein. From 1959 to 1961 there were several more attempts on his life. Thereafter things appeared to settle down for a while, with peace being made with Egypt in 1961; this was followed by an increase in national prosperity.

In 1963, Syria, Iraq, and Egypt signed an agreement for the formation of a "loose" union, and this unleashed massive demonstrations in Jordan both for and against the union. Turmoil became so great that King Hussein dissolved parliament and declared martial law. The crackdown, however, did not bring peace to the country.

THE PALESTINIAN LIBERATION ORGANIZATION

The PLO had its early beginnings in 1951 in Cairo, Egypt. Formed by Palestinian students, its five main goals were the liberation of Palestine, the need for armed struggle to attain this goal, reliance on self-organization, cooperation with friendly Arab forces, and cooperation with sympathetic international forces. The new organization, headed by Yasser Arafat,

Palestinian opposition to the new state of Israel was formalized with the creation of the PLO in 1964, with Yasser Arafat (above) as its leader. The PLO, however, did not have the support of King Hussein and there was much tension between the Jordanian government and the PLO over the latter's use of Jordan to launch its attacks against Israel.

realized that it could not depend to any significant degree on Arab countries and set out to fight its battles in its own ways. These included surprise raids on Israeli settlements and terrorist acts against government installations and citizens of Western countries that heavily supported Israel at the expense of the Palestinian people.

It was only in 1964 that the organization was formed officially and a charter established in Jerusalem, which at that time was part of Jordan. Shortly after, the PLO established its headquarters in Amman, and a rocky relationship began between Jordan's government and the PLO. By 1965 tension was rising between King Hussein and the PLO over the latter's use of Jordan as a base to attack Israel, which resulted in Israeli reprisals against Jordanian villages. The king then forced the closing of the PLO office in Amman. In 1967 an Israeli attack on a Jordanian village as a reprisal for a PLO attack from Jordan set off the 1967 Arab-Israeli war. The war lasted only three days and the winner, Israel, took the West Bank from Jordan.

A Jordanian-based PLO action against Israel in 1968 caused Israeli reprisals against Jordanian villages and created internal pressure on the government to control the PLO. For a long time the organization laid low,

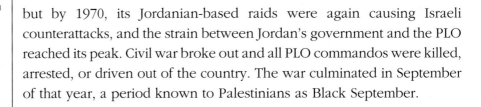

but by 1970, its Jordanian-based raids were again causing Israeli counterattacks, and the strain between Jordan's government and the PLO reached its peak. Civil war broke out and all PLO commandos were killed, arrested, or driven out of the country. The war culminated in September of that year, a period known to Palestinians as Black September.

TOWARD MODERN TIMES

"For some time to come, the stability of the Arab state will continue to rest on the ability of political leadership to exercise effective control through coercion."

—*Arabist scholars Adeeb Dawisha and I. William Zartman*

In 1973 another Arab-Israeli war broke out and more Palestinian refugees flooded into Jordan. Then from 1980 to 1983 war with Syria was narrowly averted over King Hussein's support of Islamic militants trying to overthrow the Syrian government. The Arab League (a council of the leaders of the Arab nations) intervened, and the king met the Syrian president and pledged to stop his country's support for the Syrian insurgents.

In 1984, with relative peace, the king resumed parliament for the first time in 21 years. He formally ceded Jordan's claim on the West Bank in 1988, paving the way for the Palestinians to stake their claim on the disputed area. For a time Jordan prospered, but the Gulf War broke out in 1991. Jordan remained neutral, but as a result of its stand, lost its aid from both Western countries and the rich Arab Gulf states.

King Hussein and Israeli Prime Minister Yitzhak Rabin signed a peace agreement in the United States in 1994.

NEW ELECTIONS LAW

In 1993 a new elections law was passed that granted multiparty democracy. Fifteen political parties formed quickly and vied for election. In 1994, after several years of secret negotiations supported by the governments and diplomats of several Western countries, Jordan and Israel declared that they could coexist peacefully.

HISTORICAL HIGHLIGHTS SINCE THE 1960S

1963   Syria, Iraq, and Egypt sign an agreement for a loose union. There are demonstrations in Jordan both for and against the move, and King Hussein dissolves parliament.

1964   The Palestinian Liberation Organization (PLO) establishes the Palestinian National Charter in Jerusalem, in the West Bank, and sets up its headquarters in Amman.

1965   Tensions rise between King Hussein and the PLO over the latter's use of Jordan as an attack base against Israel. The Jordanian army kills a PLO commando after a PLO raid on Israel.

1966   King Hussein closes the PLO offices in Amman.

1967   An Israeli attack on a Jordanian village (a reprisal for a PLO attack from Jordan) destroys the village and kills or injures 60 Jordanians, setting off the 1967 Arab-Israeli war. Israel takes the West Bank from Jordan and the Arab world mourns the loss of Jerusalem, Islam's second most holy city, to Israel.

1967–1968 There is growing trouble with King Hussein's moderate stance toward Israel and a rapidly increasing Palestinian population. Jordanian-based PLO action against Israel results in Israeli reprisals against Jordanian villages and creates internal pressure to control the PLO. The Jordanian army kills 28 PLO commandos.

1970   The strain between Jordan and the PLO reaches a peak. A civil war breaks out—including battles with Syria, which supports the PLO—and all commandos are killed, arrested, or driven out of the country. The event is known to Palestinians as "Black September" as fighting continued through most of September.

1973   Another Arab-Israeli war breaks out. Jordan does not fight but sends troops and equipment to help Syria. More Palestinian refugees flood into Jordan.

1980–1983 A war with Syria is narrowly averted. The cause of trouble is King Hussein's support of Islamic militants trying to overthrow the Syrian government. The Arab League intervenes. King Hussein meets the Syrian president and promises to stop his country's support for the insurgents.

1984   Parliament resumes for the first time in 21 years.

1986   A new electoral law is passed, creating small constituencies—Christians, Palestinians, and Circassians/Chechens. The Palestinians in refugee camps are also given representation.

1988   King Hussein formally cedes Jordan's claim on the West Bank to the Palestinians.

1991   The Gulf War breaks out. Jordan remains neutral and loses much aid from both Western countries and rich Arab Gulf countries. It is flooded with refugees from Iraq and Palestinians from Kuwait.

1993   A new elections law is passed and 15 political parties take part in elections.

1994   Jordan and Israel declare peaceful coexistence at ceremonies in the White House in Washington, D.C.

GOVERNMENT

JORDAN'S OFFICIAL NAME IS The Hashemite Kingdom of Jordan. Despite its past turmoil and long-term suspension of parliament and civil liberties, it is generally considered to have the most democratic Arab government today. Its bureaucracy, although huge, is one of the most efficient and least corrupt in the Arab world.

GOVERNMENT STRUCTURE

The monarch is head of state, while a prime minister appointed by the king heads the day-to-day affairs of government. The prime minister appoints a cabinet. Both the prime minister and cabinet are subject to parliamentary approval.

The legislative assembly, or parliament, has 142 members and is divided into two houses: a senate whose members are appointed by the king, and a house of representatives whose members are elected by popular vote. A term of office lasts four years. All citizens over 18 (except members of the royal family) can vote, including Palestinians in refugee camps. The monarch signs and executes or vetoes all laws passed by parliament, as well as any constitutional amendments. He is also the commander of the armed forces.

Above: **Men carrying the Jordanian flag.**

Opposite: **The Hashemite coat of arms located at the main entrance of a fort in Aqaba.**

Under the central government are five territorial districts called *muhafaza* ("mu-HAH-fah-zah"), each headed by a governor appointed by the minister of interior. Under the district governments are cities and towns, each with a popularly elected mayor and council responsible for local affairs.

39

When King Hussein assumed the throne in 1953, he inherited a poor and divided country. Years later, however, he had succeeded in building an independent nation with its own identity.

THE MONARCH   Unlike most countries with royal leaders who are descendants of hundreds or thousands of years of family rule, Jordan's royalty is a creation of 20th century forces, specifically British will and the overpowering desire of Abdullah ibn Hussein to be king. This situation is unique to the Muslim world, where being descended from the Prophet Mohammed, because of the nature of Islam, is all that is needed to become a supreme ruler. Abdullah's father (King Hussein's great-grandfather) was such a leader—but not in the territory that is now Jordan.

King Hussein claims (and most Arabs accept) that he is a descendant of the Prophet Mohammed via the house of Hashem ("HAH-shim") from the tribe of Qureish ("ku-RAYSH")—hence, the country's official name of "The Hashemite Kingdom of Jordan." His ancestry is one of the reasons he has remained in power in a land that his family was not part of only two generations before.

KINGS, CITIZENS, AND DEBTS

King Hussein is known for his largesse. Citizens can make personal requests of him at his palaces, and such requests are most often from the poorest, least important citizens. Palace personnel screen the requests to eliminate those that are too onerous, but most are granted. This makes the recipients and their families indebted to the king and gains their support. Likewise, King Hussein considers himself in debt to anyone who is harmed by a member of the royal family and invites them to make a request for recompense (compensation for personal injury is a common characteristic of Arab culture). Most people ask only for something simple such as a photograph of themselves with the king.

The monarch also regularly visits tribal groups, providing feasts for them from royal coffers, thereby indebting them to him further. In describing the concept of nation, the scholar Linda Layne has said: "Because spaces, whether domestic or national, are defined by people and not by places, they are not permanent or fixed. It is the social action of individuals that makes both house and homeland."

Only a few decades ago, Jordan was little more than a barren land with a few Bedouin tribes grazing their sheep. So to a large extent, it is through the social actions of the monarch that it has become a genuine nation. The king is a man with modern ideas who believes in diplomacy rather than military action. Although his government has been repressive at times, such action, he felt, was necessary to stave off anarchy in a volatile culture. The country's culture is still heavily influenced by the philosophy of clan loyalty, personal retaliation, and powerful religious and political beliefs that are often backed up by violent action.

Crown Prince Hassan, King Hussein's brother, heads the National Center for Educational Research and Development.

Although the first-born son of a king or queen traditionally accedes to the throne, Jordan's monarch may change that accession by decree. King Hussein has selected his younger brother Hassan as crown prince. There can only be speculation as to why the king has done this, but it may have something to do with the fact that his children have several different mothers, two of whom are Westerners.

WESTERN QUEENS IN THE DESERT

Muslim men, by both law and custom, are allowed to have up to four
wives. King Hussein has married four women, but only one at a time. It
is believed that he divorced his first wife, Dina Abdul Hamed (an Arab),
because she tried to become politically powerful at his expense. After the
divorce, the king traveled a great deal in Europe where he met and
eventually married a British woman, Toni Gardner. She converted to the
Muslim faith, took the name of Muna, and bore the king four children.

In 1973, King Hussein divorced Muna and almost immediately announced
his engagement to a beautiful young Jordanian Palestinian, Alia Toukan,
who worked for Royal Jordanian Airlines. Jordanians were extremely
upset, as Queen Muna had been popular with most of them, and the king
was criticized harshly in the press—not for marrying the younger woman,
but for divorcing the older one. One paper condemned his "typical male
Arab attitude" toward women.

In the winter of 1977, Queen Alia was killed in a helicopter crash in the
hills of the Jordan Valley. The king mourned her loss, but just a year later
met a Princeton-educated American named Lisa Halaby, who had ancestors
from Allepo in Syria. They were married a few months later after she had

converted to Islam and was renamed Noor al-Hussein, or Light of Hussein. For the second time, an Arab country has had a queen from the West, both of whom have endeared themselves to the native citizens.

MINORITY GROUP REPRESENTATION

Jordan's election laws guarantee that minority groups are represented. First, the constitution outlaws any discrimination based on race, language, or religion. Heads of state and prime ministers, however, must be Muslim. This is not an unreasonable requirement considering the fact that more than 90% of the populace is Muslim. Christians, who make up only 6% of Jordan's population, are accorded 17 legislative members, or 12% of parliament. Circassians and Chechens are granted one legislative seat for every 5,000 citizens, compared to one for every 27,000 Muslims. Bedouins who still live a traditional, nomadic lifestyle account

All citizens above the age of 18 are eligible to vote.

for only 1% of the population but are guaranteed legislative representation that is even more out of proportion than that of the Christians, Circassians, and Chechens. Even Palestinians in refugee camps are granted representation in parliament.

Although such representation might seem unfair to the majority, it is the king's and government's way of protecting the rights and interests of small groups against an often volatile majority.

LAW, ORDER, AND PROTECTION

Jordan's military, police, and legal systems are based upon modern British models.

Jordanian soldiers patrol the country as well as its border with Israel. In 1991, Jordan became the only Arab country to scrap compulsory military service.

MILITARY The Jordanian army has 75,000 members; the air force, about 11,000; the naval coast guard, a few hundred; and the "people's militia," in which women can serve, about 15,000. This is one of the smallest militaries in the Arabian peninsula and is only a fraction of the size of Syria's and Iraq's military organizations, each of which has more than a million members. Despite its small size, Jordan's military absorbs one-quarter of the national budget. It is well-trained and dedicated to the government. King Hussein is the commander-in-chief.

POLICE The regular police force is modern and limited in authority by the constitution, but Jordan, like every other Arab country, has a "secret" police that can infiltrate and control groups the government feels are a threat to its survival. In the past the secret police have been brutally repressive, engaging in torture, midnight arrests, and even murder. Since the early 1990s, however, the force has been reined in substantially and now serves a function more similar to the American FBI or British Scotland Yard. Old habits die hard, though, and abuses still exist.

"CAMEL" POLICE Jordan has a special police branch called the Desert Patrol or Camel Corps whose function is to patrol the desert, giving assistance to desert dwellers. It was established in 1931 to help keep the peace among warring tribes, but today, with a decline in the traditional Bedouin lifestyle, it exists more out of tradition than from real need. These police wear khaki uniforms and red-and-white headdresses called *kaffiyeh* ("kah-FEE-yay"), and carry handcrafted silver daggers in silver scabbards. Today the Camel Corps has about 1,000 members.

THE LEGAL SYSTEM Judges are appointed by the king, and there are three categories of courts: regular, civil, and criminal. These include the Supreme Court; Muslim and Christian courts to address personal matters such as inheritance and marriage; and special courts for land, municipal, tax, and customs issues.

The legal system protects the interests of Jordan's minority citizens. Christians have their own courts for personal and civic matters, and the ancient tribal laws of the Bedouins take precedence over the legal system in their own affairs. The Circassians and Chechens use the Islamic courts. Jordan's laws are based in part on Islamic precepts (particularly in courts for Muslims), but Jordan does not follow the Shari'a ("shah-REE-ah")—Islamic law—as do Saudi Arabia and a few other predominantly Muslim countries.

The camel-mounted Desert Patrol is a welcome sight to travelers who venture too far into the desert with too little water or who get lost in its vastness.

The Shari'a requires punishments that most modern people consider barbaric, such as amputation of the hand of a thief; the death penalty for anyone who has sexual relations outside of marriage; and the death penalty for anyone who "blasphemes" the Prophet Mohammed, the Koran, or Islam.

ECONOMY

JORDAN HAS FEW NATURAL RESOURCES, land that is largely too dry for raising crops, and industries that are mostly newly developed, yet it has achieved a moderately strong, modern economy and is beginning to support itself financially. It also receives extensive financial aid from Britain and the United States.

After Jordan's loss of the West Bank to Israeli forces during the 1967 Arab-Israeli war, there were fears that its economic development would be impeded. However, it has overcome the setback and the country's economy continues to expand. In 1990 per capita gross national product (GNP) was US$1,340; it fell to US$968 following the Gulf War in 1991. This does not compare favorably with neighboring Israel's per capita GNP of US$11,878, but the Jordanians still enjoy a fairly high standard of living. Average income, for example, increased by 300% from 1954 to 1966. The country has the second largest stock market in the Arab world, after Kuwait.

Above: **The Housing Bank Center in Amman.**

Opposite: **Another bank in Amman. Until the time of the Gulf War in 1991, the country's income was boosted by remittances from Jordanians and Palestinians working in the Gulf States.**

Although oil is yet to be found in commercial amounts, the government is putting its hopes on natural gas reserves found in 1987 in the northeastern part of the country. These reserves now supply 15% of Jordan's energy needs.

The economy has been growing steadily since the Gulf War—11% in 1992 and 6% in 1993. In 1994 exports increased 23% over the previous year. Banking has become a strong and growing service industry.

Members of the Druze ethnic minority collecting salt.

MINING AND MANUFACTURING

Jordan's industrial output provides most of its GNP (27%) and exports (47%). Its industrial base consists primarily of small plants, few of which employ high-technology methods. Larger, heavy industries are either part of the public sector or heavily supported by the government. Mining provides the largest single share of the country's domestic economy. This is mostly phosphate and potash from the Dead Sea. Salt, limestone (used in making cement), gypsum, and marble are also mined. The country's major industries for domestic production are paper and cardboard (using imported wood chips), detergents, phosphates, alcoholic drinks, and petroleum refining.

Jordan's major trading partners are its Arab neighbors, predominantly Saudi Arabia. Its main exports, in order of sales volume, are chemicals, phosphates, and manufactured goods such as machinery and transport equipment. Its main imports are food products, livestock feed, manufacturing equipment, and consumer goods that come from Germany, Britain, the United States, Italy, and Japan.

AGRICULTURE

Less than 10% of Jordan's land is arable. Because of this, agriculture accounts for a tiny part of its economy and exports. The main products are wheat, barley, maize, millet, lentils, beans, peas, sesame, tobacco, tomatoes, cucumbers, citrus (mostly lemons), melons, cabbages, potatoes, onions, and bananas. Modern methods have greatly increased productivity, and most of the vegetables are exported.

Although the most common farm animals are sheep, goats, and chickens, the latter is the only livestock the country can produce enough of to satisfy domestic demand; it produces less than 30% of its beef and lamb requirements. There is a small fishing industry in the Red Sea. Despite the popular image of Arabs perched on camels, there are few camels in Jordan, mostly among the Bedouins and in the Camel Corps. The commonest work animals are donkeys and horses.

Forestation is a high priority of the government; seedlings are provided to farmers free of charge. The only natural forests are those on some hills of the Jordan River Valley and in some areas on the high plateau.

Lettuce harvest in the Jordan River Valley.

A swim in the Dead Sea is popular with tourists. The high density water makes it impossible to sink.

TOURISM

When the West Bank was part of Jordan, tourism was the country's largest single source of income. But with the 1967 loss of the West Bank and its main tourist attraction, the ancient and holy city of Jerusalem, that income is gone. Nevertheless, Jordan receives about two million tourists annually. Most are from the wealthier Arab countries, and tourism provides more foreign exchange than all the country's exports combined.

Jordan also has the highest proportion of Western tourists of any Arab country except for Egypt, and the recently signed peace accord with Israel is likely to increase tourism substantially. Shortly after King Hussein met the late Israeli prime minister Yitzhak Rabin in Washington, D.C., the press in Jordan publicized the few Israelis who immediately traveled to Jordan. In one case, a television camera crew trailed an Israeli woman and her daughter who were visiting southern Jordan, recording their positive reactions to what they saw and the hospitality they experienced, as well as the favorable reactions of some Jordanians whom the visitors encountered.

The ruins of former civilizations (particularly those of Petra); the stark, pristine beauty of the desert; and the coastal resort area of Aqaba are likely to draw larger numbers of visitors in the future.

JOBS

About 45% of Jordan's labor force work in social and administrative services, mostly for the government. Another 20% work in construction, mining, and manufacturing. These include factories involved in milling, brewing, oil pressing, canning, and furniture-making, as well as the pharmaceutical and cement factories. Less than 10% work in agriculture. Most of the remaining 25% work in service industries, of which banking is the strongest. Egyptians are a large percentage of the tourism workers in southern Jordan.

Although wages are low by Western standards, so are prices. Compare the buying power of an average middle-aged bank worker in Jordan with one in Syria, for example. The worker in Syria is paid the equivalent of US$80–100 a month, while the worker in Jordan is paid around US$1,000 a month. A car in Syria is beyond the wildest dreams of the bank worker— a 10-year-old economy model costs more than US$10,000—while a car of the same model and age in Jordan will cost only US$2,000–3,000. The Syrian worker in Damascus trying to find a new apartment in the central city will find asking prices of US$100,000 and more for very modest places, while the Jordanian can find one in Amman for less than half that amount.

However, some things do cost more. If these two workers stop on the street to buy a *shawarma* ("shah-WAHR-mah"), a burrito-type sandwich, the Syrian will pay about US50 cents; the Jordanian will pay about US$1.50.

Jordan's population is one of the best educated in the Arab world, and many of the lowest-paying jobs are done by Egyptian laborers, at least some of whom are in the country illegally. In 1991 Jordan had 17 trade unions, and there are industrial courts to handle trade disputes. Physicians' and engineers' associations control licensing of those professions.

In the late 1980s the estimated number of foreign workers in Jordan stood at 200,000, half of whom were Egyptian. Most of the remainder were Sri Lankan, Filipino, Pakistani, and Indian, all of whom were domestic workers. There were also some highly skilled personnel from Western countries— predominantly technicians and teachers.

ECONOMIC PROBLEMS

Jordan has numerous economic difficulties. In 1991 total exports stood at US$29.8 million, while imports cost US$66.2 million—and there has always been a similar trade deficit. In 1991 the national debt stood at 1.2 billion Jordanian dinars, or US$1.6 billion. The economy has to support nearly a million Palestinian and Iraqi refugees. Population growth has been close to 4% annually, 52% of the population is under 15 years of age, and 75% is under 30. Also, the unemployment rate, which was 8% in 1986, had increased to 19% by 1991.

TRANSPORTATION

Jordan has about 3,100 miles (4,990 km) of developed roads that connect major cities and towns and provide land routes to neighboring countries. Two routes south of Amman lead to Aqaba: the Desert Highway and King's Highway. The Allenby Bridge is the main highway across the Jordan River for those traveling to the West Bank. The original Hejaz railroad built by the Ottomans has been rebuilt and expanded. The port in Aqaba is small but handles several million tons of goods annually and is the terminus of an oil pipeline for Iraqi oil.

Old and new modes of transport make a striking contrast.

The country's only airline, Royal Jordanian Air (Alia), is profitable and one of the best in the Mediterranean basin. It serves Jordan out of the single international airport outside Amman, but there is also a small airport in Aqaba. The national bus service, JETT, is inexpensive and efficient and includes several runs daily to Damascus in Syria, about 200 miles (320 km) from Amman. The most common taxi vehicle is the Mercedes Benz.

WHAT UNEMPLOYMENT FIGURES DO NOT SHOW

In 1987, when Jordan's unemployment rate stood at 8%, there were about 325,000 Jordanians working abroad. With the level of unemployment that is common now, that figure has nearly doubled, and will most likely continue to climb as the baby boomers of the past 20 years come of age. As the population of young adults grows, a shortage of jobs will be keenly felt. Such a situation often creates severe social unrest as the young people from wealthy families can go abroad for their university education and find work overseas, or return to good jobs at home. Meanwhile the poorer youths, left behind without jobs or hope, can be recruited by radical or violent leaders (some of whom belong to religious groups) hungry for political power. This sort of situation has occurred in Egypt, Algeria, Pakistan, and Bangladesh and can happen in many other poor countries where the population has increased rapidly.

The long-term prospects for societies that are unable or unwilling to control their population growth are not good. Despite the efforts of Jordan's government in pushing for smaller families, it is fighting against powerful tradition and religious beliefs.

Professional jobs may be harder to come by, but life goes on in the thriving marketplace as it has for centuries.

JORDANIANS

JORDAN HAS THE MOST HOMOGENEOUS POPULATION of any Arab country, both ethnically and religiously. All but a handful of its population is Arab, and the primary difference is between urban and rural, Palestinian and Bedouin. Usually Palestinian-Jordanians are the urban residents, while the rural people are Bedouins.

POPULATION STATISTICS

Like all Arab countries, Jordan has suffered a population explosion since World War II. Its annual growth rate has been almost 4% over the past three decades. A big part of this growth is the result of high birth rates, but refugees from both Palestine and Iraq have contributed greatly at certain times. In fact, people of Palestinian origin account for about 60% of Jordan's population.

In 1921, just before Jordan became a country, the population was 230,000. In 1938 the estimated population was 300,000—many of them Palestinian refugees fleeing violence in Palestine. In 1952 there were 680,000 people in the country, nearly half of them Palestinians expelled from the new Jewish country of Israel. In 1979 the population reached 2.1 million. In 1990 there were 3.2 million residents; only a year later, the population swelled to 4.1 million, due in part to an inflow of Iraqi refugees from the Gulf War and Jordanian workers returning from Iraq and Kuwait. Today, there are about 4.3 million people in Jordan. In spite of differing ideologies between the various groups of people, the government has sought to promote a sense of national loyalty.

Opposite: **Couple at the University of Jordan Recreation Center. The educated young are often seen in Western-style clothes.**

Below: **Bedouin children in Petra.**

Street stall in the older part of town reflects the lifestyle and pursuits of the common people.

RACE AND CLASS

Palestinians are better educated, more Westernized in social characteristics, and generally more sophisticated than any other Arab group. These things have made them a bit more egalitarian than other Arabs, and since the majority of Jordanians are Palestinian, the country has less obvious racism than in many other Arab countries. Class consciousness, however, is common. No matter how much wealth one has, it is how one shows it that counts. There is not much socializing between the upper and lower classes as there might be in North America, for example. Educated city dwellers feel superior toward illiterate villagers and the Bedouins.

Manual labor of any kind is thought to be beneath the dignity of anyone in the upper classes. The majority of wealthy Jordanians, for example, employ foreign servants to do the household chores. The general attitude is that these people are inferior to Arabs. Likewise, Arabs from poorer countries such as Yemen and Egypt are also considered inferior. The urban Palestinians also scorn what they think is the archaic tribalism and crude customs of the Bedouins.

The older, wealthy Jordanians have little desire to own the beautiful, traditional handicrafts made in Jordan. Instead, they prefer something made in the United States or Europe.

DRESSING

Most Jordanians dress in Western fashions. Generally, only the Bedouins and some villagers wear more traditional garb such as the *kaffiyeh* and various gowns. At night and in colder weather a heavy, sleeveless coat may be worn.

Many women wear scarves and full-length, long-sleeved dresses, but these have a modern look with bright colors and snug fits. In some communities the women take great pride in their embroidery skills, displayed on their everyday clothes. Girls learn such skills at an early age.

Middle- and upper-class women like bright colors, elaborate designs, lots of jewelry and makeup, high-heeled shoes, and long hair that is heavily coifed. Blue jeans, T-shirts, running shoes, and other such casual dress are also common, especially among teenagers. Young men of the middle- and upper-classes usually wear short hair and are very dressy.

Few Jordanians—only very Westernized youths—wear shorts, mini-skirts, short hair (for women or girls), or long hair (for men). Others are often torn between their cultural heritage and influences from the West. Many younger adults, however, are beginning to develop an appreciation for their ancestors' traditional dress and wear them on special occasions. Devout Muslim women rarely expose more than their hands, ankles, and sometimes face.

Women generally prefer bright colors and richly embroidered designs created with colored thread.

Above: **Meal time for children in a Palestinian refugee camp.**

Opposite: **Bedouin men sit on the ground in a circle, drinking coffee and talking about the day's events.**

MINORITY GROUPS

More than half the population are Palestinians, while descendants of the traditional Bedouins comprise most of the rest. There are a few minority groups in Jordan.

PALESTINIAN REFUGEES It seems illogical to categorize these as a minority when Palestinians are the majority in the country. But there is a distinction between those who have integrated into Jordanian society, become economically successful, and hold no hope of returning to their former homeland, and others who live in refugee camps. The latter are usually first generation refugees and their children. Both the settled Palestinians and refugees enjoy full Jordanian citizenship, and the latter are termed "refugees" primarily to gain them assistance—medically, economically, and socially—from the United Nations Refugee and Works Agency. While there is no racial difference between the two, the integrated, successful Palestinians often feel superior to the refugees.

BEDOUINS It is ironic that the Bedouins, who were the only inhabitants of Jordan's land outside the East Bank just a few generations ago, are now a minority group. They can be distinguished from other Arabs by their shorter, thinner bodies, and smaller, pointed facial features.

Only 1% of Jordan's population now live in tents, but there is still a romantic image in the hearts of many Arabs of the strong and independent nomad, and the goat-hair tent provides a visual image of that romance.

Strips of goat's wool 24–32 inches (60–80 cm) wide are woven outdoors on looms. The work is done by Bedouin women. Six to eight of these strips are then sewn together, making each tent between 12 and 15 feet (3.7 and 4.6 m) wide. The length of a tent may vary, but the width remains the same. Center poles 10–13 feet (3–4 m) apart divide the tent into "rooms" with the help of woven "walls" 3–5 feet (1–1.5 m) high. Most tents have two such rooms: one where the women sleep and one for the men. Extended families may have three, with an extra room for a son's family. Only sheikhs (tribal leaders) have tents with four to five rooms, since great hospitality is expected of them when people come to visit.

Living in a tent that is larger than what a family needs is considered pretentious and increases the demand for hospitality because tent size indicates wealth and position. The interiors of most village houses are designed like those of the tents.

Their Arabic name, *Badoo* ("BAH-doo"), means "desert dweller" and comes from the same Arabic root word as *badiya* ("BAH-dee-yah"), which means "desert" or "steppe." They are traditionally a nomadic people, and before the advent of modernization, camels were their main means of transport. Without camels, the Bedouins would have found it difficult to survive in the desert. The camel is ideally suited to life in the desert because it can store enough water in its hump to last up to 15 days. It also has reserves of fat in its hump so that it can go without food for several days. The largest Bedouin groups are the Bani Sukhurs, Huwayatats, and Sirhans.

Despite the erosion of the Bedouins' traditional lifestyle, many elements of their culture live on in the daily lives of most Jordanians: segregation of genders, arranged marriages, loyalty to clan, submission to a strong and autocratic leader, belief in harsh punishments, a strict code of honor, and warm hospitality.

CIRCASSIANS AND CHECHENS In the 1880s, the Russian tsar sent troops to invade the small central-Asian area now called Chechnya in a form of crusade against the Muslims there. In order to save some of their fellow believers, the Ottomans resettled several thousand Circassians and Chechens—two separate tribes—in Transjordan.

The Circassians were established in the area of Amman, then the ruins of the once-prosperous Roman city of Philadelphia. They rebuilt the city, established the manufacturing city of Zarqa, and introduced large-wheeled carts and a system of dirt roads in the Amman-Zarqa area. The fact that these refugees were transplanted into Jordan seems ominous in retrospect: refugees and their descendants now have a sizeable presence in the country. The Circassians, with their industrious character, also established an economic pattern that continues today.

THE POWER OF LEGENDS

In traditional Arab culture, legends were standards to be lived up to. Here is the story of Hatim at-Tay, relating to Arab hospitality.

Before his birth, Hatim's mother had a dream in which she had the choice of having 10 sons as brave as eagles, or one who would surpass all men in generosity. She chose the latter. One day early in his life, Hatim was sent to pasture the family's camels. He returned soon after, happily saying that he had brought fame to his ancestral name by giving away all the camels as gifts.

Years later, after Hatim's death, a rival tribe that was jealous of his reputation was camping near his grave and scorning his deeds. During the night he appeared in a dream to the leader of the group, inviting the man to feast on his tribe's only camel. In the morning the man discovered that his camel was dead, so the tribe did feast on it.

As the people went on their way after breakfast, they met Hatim's son leading a black camel. He told the tribe that his father had appeared in a dream the night before and ordered him to find the tribe traveling without a camel so that he could give it the black one.

This group is well-integrated into society, with high government and business positions, although socially they maintain a certain distance from the Arabs. There are about 25,000 of them today, and they have their own language and culture.

The Chechens also have their own language and culture but have not been as economically successful as the Circassians. Except for a few Iraqi refugees, they are the only Shi'ite Muslims in Jordan, and their current population numbers only about 2,500.

CHRISTIANS This group is a minority only with respect to religion: they are all Arabs and hold most of the same cultural characteristics of the general population. The Christians have never been persecuted in Jordan and are, in fact, allies of the government, not opponents. They hold many positions in government, education, and business and—like the Circassians—are among the most prosperous and best-educated citizens. They constitute about 6% of the population.

Most Christians belong to the Eastern Orthodox and Greek Catholic churches, but there are some Roman Catholics and Protestants as well. They trace the roots of their religion back to the pre-Islamic era when Christianity was founded in the region and later upheld by the Roman rulers. Near the border with Syria there is a group of Samaritans who are descendants of an ancient Jewish sect.

Jordanian Christian family. The women generally do not wear the long gowns and head coverings that distinguish Muslim women.

Hospitality is a byword among Arabs, whatever their station in life … When they say, as they often do, "My home is your home," they mean it.

—Margaret K. Nydell, Arabist scholar

ATTITUDE TOWARD FOREIGNERS

While hospitality is the norm among all Arabs, educated city dwellers seem to have lost much of the almost overwhelming hospitality that is still so common among the Bedouins and villagers. A small shopkeeper, however, will serve tea or coffee to anyone who comes by, and most people will also be helpful when a visitor is in trouble or has any sort of problem. Assistance to a needy outsider is deeply ingrained in Arab consciousness.

In the desert and villages it is still common for travelers to be invited into a Bedouin tent or a village house for tea or coffee. Many questions will be asked of the visitor as most people, especially the children, are very curious about foreigners. Despite the general friendliness, there are some characteristics of Jordanian culture that disturb many outsiders.

STARING In Arab culture it is not a challenge for one man to stare at another as it would be in the United States, for example. It is also not considered rude for men to stare intensely at a woman, even if she is with another man. Often the intensity and duration of the stare is most upsetting, and if the foreigner stares back, the Arab will not be embarrassed and may actually strike up a conversation with the visitor. The greatest interest is directed toward light-haired, fair-skinned people.

LACK OF PERSONAL SPACE In Arab culture there is no concept of personal public space. When people are in public they can expect to get jostled, and this applies to foreigners as well. Even bumping into another person is not considered rude and apologies are seldom offered.

PERSONAL QUESTIONS Many Jordanians are very curious about foreigners and ask personal questions of them. They do not understand if a visitor is reluctant to answer some of the questions, particularly with regard to marital status and family matters.

The older cities are crowded and jostling is common. The Arabs are a social people and the concept of personal privacy does not exist. The Arabic word that comes closest to "privacy" is one that would be translated in English as "loneliness."

CHANGING ATTITUDES This is most marked among the rural people. The changes are seen in many aspects of their daily life. Many men, for example, now wear trousers bought at the souk (open-air marketplace) but still keep their traditional headgear.

Even nomadic Bedouins are collecting more possessions, and this makes it difficult for them to move from place to place. As a result families now prefer not to change campsites for as long as they can.

Another change is that fewer camels are kept, as alternative modes of transport are available. Many camel herders have turned to keeping sheep, which are easier to tend. Today not all nomads are whole families on the move. Many individuals are paid to look after camels or sheep belonging to others.

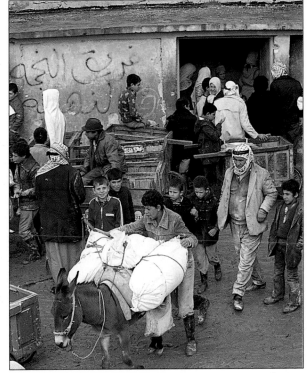

LIFESTYLE

THE LIFESTYLE OF JORDAN'S WEALTHY, college-educated, city dwellers is different from that of the less-educated, rural people. However, they all share a love for socializing. The rhythm of life is set by the call to prayer five times a day, the late start in the morning to the day's activities (generally around 9 or 10 a.m.), the mid-afternoon lunch and extended rest period while the intense heat of midday passes (usually from 1 p.m. to 4 or 5 p.m.), and late nights. Most shops stay open until 9 or 10 p.m., and Jordanians do not eat dinner until after 8 p.m.

Wealthy Jordanians travel a lot, and most have been to North America and Europe. They also have relatives who live in these places. In Jordan, they live in extravagant homes (what Americans would call luxury condominiums); drive expensive new cars; hire domestic help to clean, cook, and help raise their children; and wear the latest Western fashions. The wealthy, urban Palestinians, in particular, seem to like all things Western.

Opposite: **Shopkeeper in Amman.**

Below: **Even the Bedouins have adapted to some "foreign" ways and shaking hands is now common, sometimes replacing the traditional embrace.**

SOCIALIZING

A traveler who visits Jordan for the first time will notice the energy the residents put into personal relationships. It is obvious on the streets and in homes, schools, and offices. Friends greet each other emotionally, with both parties talking at the same time. They ask about each other's families, work or studies, and health, and always extend an invitation to the other party to visit them at home and have tea or coffee. Then they say goodbye in several ways, always bestowing blessings on each other.

Jordanians are comfortable with just being part of the hustle and bustle of life. No one likes to stand out too much in a crowd.

PHYSICAL CLOSENESS Part of Arab social intensity is shown by physical closeness: male friends hug and kiss each other and women do the same. Jordanian friends touch each other frequently. Young lovers and older married people sometimes walk arm-in-arm or holding hands, but there is rarely any public emotional display between opposite genders. Few men and women or boys and girls are friends, not only because of the usual segregation that goes with Arab and Islamic culture, but also because the concept is foreign to most of them. If you are a man, your friends are men; if you are a woman, your friends are women.

CULTURAL ATTITUDES

Most Jordanians love to laugh, joke, eat, and talk. They also like loud music, car horns, loud voices, and hand-clapping. Although Amman is much quieter than Damascus or Cairo, it is quite noisy when one visits the crowded areas of the city where the lower classes live. As people become better off, children are less involved in the workforce and can enjoy the pleasures of childhood. Arabs, whether Christian or Muslim, strongly believe in fate, and that belief shows in the constant use of the word *insha'allah* ("in-SHAH-ahl-LAH," meaning "God willing") whenever they talk about the future. This "culture of fate" shows up in other ways as well. For example, they are not particularly concerned about time and schedules. Being on time does not matter because whatever is going to happen will happen anyway.

COMMON JORDANIAN CHARACTERISTICS

- Almost all men smoke.
- Few keep pets.
- People (especially men) drive very fast.
- Most Jordanians do not like to exercise.
- There is little violent crime in Jordan.
- Most men do not wear silk, diamonds, or gold; these are considered to be for women only.
- Most women do not use veils, but many wear headscarves instead.
- Men carry strings of "worry" beads, rolling the beads (made from stone, bone, or ceramic) between their fingers. Each string has 33 beads—the number of names used for God.
- In Muslim courts, fathers invariably get custody of children in a divorce.

GROUP CONFORMITY Being part of a clan is ingrained in Arab tradition. The immediate family holds first loyalty, then clan or village (sometimes these are the same), ethnic group, religion, and finally, nationality. King Hussein himself once said, "We are Arabs first and Jordanians second."

There is a certain lack of creativity among Jordanians—they do not like to stand out too much from the group. Truly original artists and writers, for example, are rare, and the naming of children is tradition-bound. Literally half the Jordanian males are named "Mohammed" ("moo-HAHM-muhd"). Many use their middle names for a little distinction. Other popular names include Ahmad ("AH-muhd"), Khalil ("kha-LEEL"), Khaled ("KHA-led"), Yassar ("yahs-SAR"), Imad ("ai-MUHD"), and Samer ("SAH-mer"). There is only a slightly larger choice of women's names.

Some modern Arab scholars lament their people's devotion to tradition at the expense of innovative and creative thinking.

GENDER SEPARATION Gender segregation and the social and familial taboos on dating create sexual naivete. Men in their 20s or even early 30s often act like adolescents in the United States when they are in the presence of women. Their intensity of feeling and behavior toward women—especially light-skinned, light-haired Westerners—often frighten the women. The concept of gender separation is so deeply ingrained that in a Bedouin family the male and female members do not eat together.

"... the Islamic system is not so much opposed to the woman as to the male-female relation itself ... such relation, if developed into an encompassing love involvement satisfying the physical, emotional, and intellectual needs of both partners, is considered as a detraction from the male's full allegiance to God."

—Issa J. Boullata, *Arabist scholar*

IMPORTANCE OF THE FAMILY

Families are the main focus of life in Jordan and children are so important
(especially sons) that fathers and mothers traditionally change their names
after the first one is born. For example, if the son is named Mahmoun, the
father becomes "Abu Mahmoun" (literally, "father of Mahmoun") and the
mother becomes "Umm Mahmoun" ("mother of Mahmoun"). If no sons are
born, the mother usually identifies herself as the mother of the first-born
daughter; fathers rarely do this, however. Most Arabs feel that being
without children and a family is very tragic.

MARRIAGES Finding a marriage partner is a preoccupation for most
Jordanians beyond their mid-teens. Arranged marriages are still the norm
in villages and among the Bedouins. Even modern city people often
cannot marry anyone they please; both families usually have to consent
to the union. First cousins still marry each other and are considered the best
match. It is quite common for the father of a young woman to approach
a young man he would like to see his daughter marry and ask if the young
man is interested. Divorces are rare, and since marriage is the main goal
in life, wedding parties are major social events.

A HOMEMADE WEDDING DRESS

Bedouins and villagers are very traditional people. One custom they practice is for a young woman to create her own wedding dress—with considerable help from older, experienced women. The patterns of the dresses are set by the village or clan tradition, although there is personal variation within those patterns. Traditional gowns are usually black and always have extensive, elaborate embroidery in patterns unique to the Palestinians. The dress takes a year or longer to sew by hand and is often "signed" by the maker: her name is embroidered onto some part of the garment. The left side of the dress is often highly decorated, while the right side only has coarse, simple designs; this is because the baby is traditionally carried on the right arm.

For tourists, such gowns are purchases prized for their intricate beauty and the tremendous amount of work that has gone into them.

DEATHS In Islam, burials cannot take place after sunset. Bodies are first washed (a man by his wife, or mother if he is unmarried; a woman usually by other women). This is a religious and social ritual during which special words are spoken for each part of the body. Muslims are not allowed to be embalmed or cremated when they die so they must be buried within hours, without clothes and wrapped in a shroud.

There are three days of mourning during which friends, relatives, and neighbors visit the family. In Muslim homes, the family is expected to feed all

Muslims believe in the resurrection of the body after death so the dead are always buried and not cremated.

guests. Women relatives wear black for many months after the death. After some time, they can start wearing a combination of black and white. For very traditional families it may be a year or longer before the women can wear other colors again. For more modern families this time is usually at least several months. If an older woman's husband dies and she does not remarry, she may wear black for the rest of her life. These traditions are similar in both Eastern Orthodox and Muslim families, although the wealthier, college-educated Palestinians do not adhere to such traditions nowadays. In traditional circles, a woman who does not fulfill the mourning traditions is harshly criticized.

In a male-dominated society such as that in Muslim countries, women are traditionally expected to tend the home and look after the children.

WOMEN'S ROLES

Women who stay single into their late 20s or beyond stand little chance of marrying anyone except perhaps a much older widower or divorced man. Such a woman is considered to be deficient in some way and will invariably continue living with her family, taking care of her aging parents. Although women are not prevented by civil law from living alone or with another woman as a roommate, they are prohibited from doing so by powerful social and family pressures.

Arab culture has always considered women to be inferior to men. Despite these traditional attitudes, the royal family and others in Jordanian society are fighting hard, but with limited access, to make the life of women better. Today, women constitute 45% of Jordan's university students and 50% of community college students, but only 11% of the workforce. Female literacy has increased from 29% in 1970 to 70% in 1990, yet the percentage of women in the workforce has remained static. Two-thirds of working women are in government jobs, half of them as teachers. About 15% work in banking.

Women can also run for political office and hold any government position. Nevertheless, there were only two appointed female members of the upper parliament, one female minister, and no judges or undersecretaries of ministries as of 1994. In 1992 twelve women ran for the Lower House of parliament but all were defeated. In 1993 three ran for office and one of them, Toujan Feisal, became the first woman elected to the House of Representatives. Finally, women have had the right to inherit land since the 1930s, but family and social pressures often dictate otherwise. The biggest social fear is that the land will pass on to strangers (the woman's husband's family) upon her death.

The government's progressive attitude will continue to bring Jordanian women into the mainstream of society. The Queen Alia and Noor al-Hussein funds help create income-generating projects for women (especially in rural areas), and in the summer of 1993 a national conference of 500 men and women from all sectors of society created the National Women's Strategy. The strategy has been formally endorsed by the government.

Women may talk of liberation in Christian society, Jewish society, or pagan society, but in Islamic society it is a grave error to speak of the liberation of women. The Muslim woman must study Islam so she will know that it is Islam that has given her all her rights.

—Zaynab al-Ghazali, founder of The Muslim Women's Association

Education is paving the way for more women to join the workforce.

EDUCATION

Jordan's literacy rate in 1961 was only 32%, but increased to 74% by 1987 and 79% by the early 1990s. Today most illiterate people are the older Jordanians—especially those in the rural areas. The aim of education is to develop the personality of each citizen, in order to bring up a generation sound in body, creed, mind, and character, and to develop citizens who work for the well-being of the country.

About 70% of primary schoolchildren attend government schools. The rest attend missionary or privately run schools.

PRIMARY AND SECONDARY SCHOOLS The Ministry of Education runs public schools, sets the curricula, and creates state examinations.

Education is compulsory through the 10th grade. Beyond that point, there is a high dropout rate. To bring its education system up-to-date, the government set up the National Center for Educational Research and Development in 1989, headed by Crown Prince Hassan.

HIGHER EDUCATION   Jordan has three state-run universities. The University of Jordan in Amman was the first, opened in 1962. Yarmuk University in Irbid was founded in 1976 and a third university in Mutah, near the southern end of the Dead Sea, opened in 1980. The universities are patterned after American universities and are often considered to be the best institutions of higher education in the Arab world. They accept international students, most of whom come from other Arab countries. There are also more than 50 technical and community colleges in addition to military institutes and a few missionary schools.

University students can study whatever they want, but the subjects taught are limited. This creates a situation that forces many students to study abroad. In the mid-1980s, for example, 60,000 Jordanians were studying overseas.

Female undergraduates heading for classes at the University of Jordan in Amman. Jordan's illiteracy rate is less than 20%, making the population one of the better-educated in the Arab region.

HEALTH

The Ministry of Health was set up in 1950 to plan the development of the country's health care service, which is high on the government's list of priorities. The cities of Amman, Zarqa, Irbid, and Aqaba have clean, well-equipped, modern hospitals with well-trained doctors and nurses, and all villages have health clinics. Some of the foreign-trained doctors speak English. A national health insurance program makes medical care affordable for all but the poorest people, who can be treated at government clinics.

The only serious infectious disease that has not been brought under control is dysentery, and most cases arise from irrigation water being contaminated by human waste. Perhaps the most serious health problem is heart disease caused by lack of exercise, heavy smoking, and high-fat diets. Life expectancy is 63 years for men and 67 years for women. The infant mortality rate is 54 deaths per 1,000 live births.

Nursing is regarded as a caring profession and is a popular career for women.

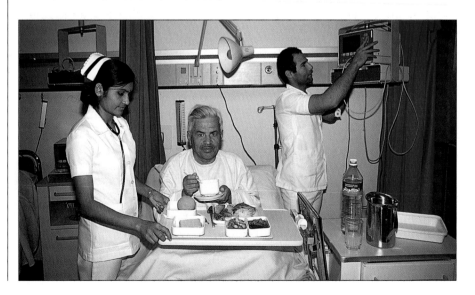

LIVING QUARTERS

Almost all residents of central Amman, Zarqa, and Irbid live in apartments. Many of them own their "houses," which Americans would call condominiums. Only members of the royal family and a few top government officials live in large, imposing, single-family homes. Villagers live in simple cottages with one to three rooms, most of which are designed after the Bedouin tent. Almost all rural residents have electricity and running water, although many do not have modern household appliances such as washing machines.

There is often a big difference between the interior furnishings and decorations of a rural home versus those of a wealthy, educated family in Amman. The rural homes have only functional furnishings that are both traditional and esthetic, whereas those of the upper classes in the city are eclectic in appearance. While furnishings, curtains, and lamps may be imported from Europe or North America, they will generally be selected for their decorative value, as Jordanians love highly ornamental surroundings. Fabrics are usually brightly-colored, frames are elaborately-carved, and chandeliers are ostentatious. Persian and Turkish carpets, especially those made of silk, are popular.

Many of the cities were built as a result of rapid expansion. Older buildings and housing developments were often erected without much thought given to planning or design.

RELIGION

JORDANIANS—MUSLIMS AND CHRISTIANS ALIKE—share a strong belief in God. They thank God for everything and leave the future up to Him. The most common response to "How are you?" is *"al Hamdulla"* ("ahl-HAHM-dool-lah"), which means literally "Thank Allah."

Today 90% of Jordan's people are Sunni Muslims (Sunni is the main branch of Islam). About 6% of the population is Christian. The country's constitution guarantees freedom of worship of all religions.

ANCIENT RELIGIONS

Before the 8th century, when the Muslim Omayyads swept across what is now Jordanian territory, there were many religions there. The Moabites, Edomites, Nabateans, Assyrians, Babylonians, Greeks, Romans, and Jews all tried to spread their own beliefs. After the death of Christ, however, most people in this land adhered to the monotheism (belief in one God) of Judaism and Christianity.

Above: **The Abu Darwish Mosque in Amman with its distinctive design.**

Opposite: **Men praying outside a mosque in Amman.**

SUNNI ISLAM

The word "Islam" means "submission to Allah." Muslims believe this is not a new religion but a continuation of Judaism and Christianity with Mohammed being the last of the prophets and the Koran (also called "The Book") superseding all other revelations from God. In the Koran, Muslims, Jews, and Christians are all referred to as "children of The Book." Even though Judaism and Christianity are native to this part of the world, Islam quickly filled the land with its beliefs.

THE STORY OF ISLAM

In A.D. 570 a man named Mohammed was born into a noble Arab family in Mecca. Muslims believe he was visited by the angel Gabriel, who gave him God's words in Arabic. The teachings were eventually compiled into the Koran. He began spreading his revelations, attracting both followers and enemies among the people of Mecca. Hostility from the Meccans drove him and his followers to Medina in 622, a migration that marks the beginning of the Muslim calendar. He returned to Mecca in 630. Although he died two years later and was buried in Medina, Mecca is Islam's holiest city, and the Kaaba ("KAH-AH-bah," a building covered with black cloth in the courtyard of the Great Mosque in Mecca), their holiest place.

Unlike Christianity, in which almost all sects have a universal leader (the Pope, for example), Islam has no hierarchy. Each mosque has a leader or *imam* ("EE-mahm")—who is a spiritual guide and lecturer by virtue of his study of Islam and his perceived piety. The Koran and the teachings of Mohammed—called the *Sunna* ("SOON-nah")—guide all aspects of Islamic life, including government, commerce, and life's daily details.

FIVE PILLARS OF ISLAM   These are the main religious principles:

1. *Shahada* ("shah-HAH-dah")—the declaration that there is only one God and that Mohammed was His last prophet.

2. *Salat* ("sah-LAHT")—prayer five times daily, at sunrise, midday, afternoon, sunset, and evening. Prayers are prescribed in both form and content. For example, the supplicant must face and bow toward Mecca, and women must cover their hair and entire bodies (except for the face, in some sects). Chanted calls to prayer are broadcast from all mosques and are part of life's daily rhythm.

3. *Zakat* ("zah-KAHT")—an annual levy of 2.5% of earnings above basic necessities. This money is used to build mosques and help the poor.

4. *Sawm* ("soom")—fasting during Ramadan, the ninth month of the Islamic year. During the fast, most Muslims do not eat, drink, or smoke from before dawn until after sunset. According to the instructions of the Koran, it begins and ends when one cannot distinguish a white thread from a black one in natural light. Those who are traveling or who fall ill during Ramadan may fast at some other time. The purposes of the fast are to purify one's soul and body and focus attention on God.

5. *Hajj* ("hahj")—the pilgrimage to Mecca. This is required at least once in a lifetime if the person can afford it. Some Muslims make the pilgrimage many times, and others pay for poorer friends and relatives to go. The *hajj* is performed during the seventh and 10th days of the 12th month of the Islamic year.

Priest outside a Christian church in Madaba.

OTHER RELIGIONS AND SECTS

Jordan's Christians are predominantly Eastern Orthodox, followed by small percentages of Greek and Roman Catholics and various Protestant sects. Near the border with Syria, there are small groups of Druze—a branch that broke off from mainstream Islam in the 10th century. Most Muslims think the Druze are heretics, and the group keeps its rituals and beliefs secret to avoid persecution.

The only Shi'ites in Jordan are the few thousand Chechens who descended from those settled there by the Ottomans, and a few hundred Iraqi refugees. Shi'ism began shortly after Prophet Mohammed died, when a group of his followers insisted someone from his family must become the Islamic leader. They chose Ali, the son of Mohammed's sister. The Sunnis believed a caliph (religious and political leader) should be elected by a council of elders. The Shi'ites are now a minority group in Islam and have some beliefs and customs that differ from those of the Sunnis. Throughout history, Shi'ites have suffered persecution from Sunnis, who believe they are heretics.

PRAYER RITUAL

The form of prayer is strictly prescribed by Islam. Supplicants first stand upright facing Mecca. The next moves are to:

- Open the hands.
- Touch the earlobes with the thumbs.
- Lower the hands and fold them, right hand over the left.
- Bow from the hips with hands on the knees.
- Straighten the body.
- Sink gently to the knees.
- Touch the ground (or floor) with hands, nose, and forehead, remaining 10–15 seconds in this position.
- Raise the body while kneeling, sitting on the heels.
- Count on the fingers.
- Press the hands, nose, and forehead to the ground again.
- Stand.

This ritual is called *raka* ("RAH-kah") and is repeated several times.

Traffic comes to a halt for Friday prayer in Amman. Friday is regarded as the holy day of the week.

LANGUAGE

ARABIC COMES FROM THE SAME ROOTS as Hebrew and other ancient tongues of the Middle East. Arabs have developed a rich oral tradition and many who are illiterate are still quite articulate. Relatively few can read classical Arabic without difficulty so the use of oral language is the ultimate art form to Arabs.

There are only two significantly different dialects in Jordan: city and rural, which is closer to standard Arabic. Educated Palestinians speak nearly the same variety as educated people in Damascus, Beirut, and Jerusalem, while villagers and the Bedouins speak a more guttural variety that more closely approximates the written forms. However, there are vast differences in spoken Arabic, so much so that educated Jordanians might have trouble understanding an Algerian, for example. Written Arabic, because of its holy status in the Koran, has changed little in 1,200 years and is written in exactly the same way in every Arabic-speaking country.

Above: **Jordanians are expressive in their speech and there is much repetition.**

Opposite: **The Koran is printed in the standard Arabic script.**

AN ANCIENT LANGUAGE

The roots of Arabic go back thousands of years to the Phoenicians. Many centuries ago Arabs trading their wares in both Africa and India spread Arabic to such an extent that some languages of both areas now share words and characteristics with Arabic—particularly in Somali and Swahili.

Private car registration plate with Arabic numerals.

A few English words are derived from Arabic as well. Examples are alcohol, algebra, check, checkmate, lute, magazine, mosaic, oud, safari, Sahara, sheriff, shish kebab, and tariff. The numerals used in Europe and North America were also originally Arabic numerals. Arabs now use numerals that came to them from India, although there is a movement favoring the use of the original Arabic numerals again.

DIFFERENT STYLES

Linguists often believe that a people's view of life is strongly influenced by the native language. If this is true, the dramatic differences between the styles of communication in Arabic and English could produce a cultural gap and conflicting views of life. Thus, it may be difficult for native speakers of either language to adjust to the speaking and writing styles of the other. This can lead to misunderstanding.

Anglo-Saxon speakers of English can often be identified by their understatement, precision, use of logic, and brevity in words: say what needs to be said very clearly and only once. Arabic speakers, on the other hand, demonstrate emotional appeal, overstatement or exaggeration, and repetition.

EMOTIONAL SPEECH Some scholars of Arab culture have said that Arabs are swayed more by words than ideas, and more by ideas than facts. Educated Anglo-Saxon English speakers are often impressed and convinced by logical arguments that contain facts and figures. An Arab, on the other hand, will usually be impressed by emotional arguments.

This difference creates communication difficulties between the two cultures. Most educated native English speakers have little regard for emotional appeals, thinking that they reflect poor taste or are a sign of low intellect. Conversely, Arabs feel that the fact-filled arguments of a Westerner, spoken with detachment, lack a human touch. Sociolinguists in the United States have found similar differences between the rhetorical styles and perceptions of some white and black Americans.

REPETITION AND HYPERBOLE Writing styles are also dramatically different in English and Arabic. Compared to most American writing, Arabic is verbose, sprinkled with colorful descriptions. Information is repeated over and over in slightly different ways. One scholar said that Arabs are forced by their culture to overstate and exaggerate in all communication or risk being misunderstood.

Overstatement is also used for the display of warmth and hospitality. If an Arabic speaker says *marhaba* ("MAR-hah-bah") or *ahlan* ("ah-LAWN")—both meaning "hello"—to another, the answer will most often be *marhabtain* ("MAR-hahb-tain") or *ahlain* ("ah-LAIN")—"two hellos"— or *ahlan wa sahlan* ("ah-LAWN wah sah-LAWN", meaning "hello and welcome"). The response outdoes the initial greeting.

WORDS IN LIEU OF ACTION Another quality of Arabic that most native English speakers fail to understand is the use of verbal threats. When Jordanians make threats, it is unlikely that they will carry out the action although people from a different culture may react adversely. On the other hand, when Jordanian enemies say nothing, there is reason to worry. In villages and among the Bedouins, "honor" and vengeance killings may occur with no warning if a family feels dishonored by the words or action of another. Such killings are illegal, but tradition lives on.

Arab conversation is peppered with blessings, which are like little prayers for good fortune, intended to keep things going well.

—*Margaret K. Nydell*

OTHER DIFFERENCES

In Arabic there is no equivalent of the English "a" and "an," but instead "al" ("ALL")—similar to the English "the"—is used with nearly all nouns, as in "Would you like the coffee?" There are also other significant grammar and sound differences between English and Arabic.

Modern Arabic publications in the style of glossy Western magazines.

TIME AND VERBS While English verbs usually indicate specific time, Arabic verbs are often not specific about time. Arabic has only a few verb forms, the main ones being past, non-past, and imperative. There are verses in the Koran, for example, in which Allah acted in both the past and future at the same time. This apparent disregard for time and chronology is reflected in day-to-day living among the Arabs. Being late for an appointment is the norm, and few people get angry when they are kept waiting. Arabic does not use a present tense form of "to be." A person who is angry, for example, would say the Arabic equivalent of "I angry."

NOUNS AND ADJECTIVES All nouns in Arabic have either male or female forms, as they do in French and Spanish. Adjectives follow nouns and must agree in both number and gender.

LANGUAGE SEXISM In English the infinitive is "to" plus a base verb; in Arabic, it is "he" plus a past tense form—for example, "he ate," or "he slept." The present-tense verb form for the third person "he" (as in "he walks") is also different from all other verb forms. For example, in the dialect used by educated city people, *behki* ("BEH-ki") means "I speak," *btehki* ("BTEH–ki") means "you speak," "she speaks," or "they speak," while *ehki* ("EH–ki") means "he speaks." The last is the form used in the dictionary. Words with associated meanings in Arabic use the same root consonants—there are words for "little boy," "children," and "giving birth" that all come from the same root. However, the word for "little girl" is unrelated. Also, the word commonly used for "son" is different than that used for "male child," while both "daughter" and "female child" are usually described by the same word.

TONGUE TWISTERS

Several Arabic letters represent sounds that English does not have. Those below show the English letter or letters usually used in transliteration (writing a language using the alphabet of a different one). While the small letters "h," "s," "d," "t," and "z" carry the same sounds as in English, writing them in capital letters produces different sounds in transliteration.

H (ha): a heavy "h" sound.

kh (kha): similar to the "ch" sound in the German "Bach." The back of the tongue against the rear roof of the mouth does not block the air flow completely.

S (sahd): a loose-tongued "s;" the tip of the tongue is not against the ridge behind the upper front teeth, but the front part of the tongue is flat against the front of the palate; somewhere between "sh" and "s" in English.

D (dahd): a loose-tongued "d;" same instructions as for *s.*

T (taa): a loose-tongued "t;" same as for *s* and *d.*

Z (zaa): a loose-tongued "z;" same as above.

9 (ayn): a vowel formed with a narrowing of the throat.

gh (ghayn): like a "g" without the back of the tongue actually touching the roof of the mouth; sometimes sounds like "l" or "r."

q (qaa): a stop like a "k," but made in the throat; Amman's dialect substitutes the hamza for this.

' (hamza): a glottal (voice box) stop usually represented in English transliterations as an apostrophe. An example is someone speaking in the Cockney dialect pronouncing bottle as "bo'le."

PROVERBS THAT ILLUSTRATE WAYS OF THINKING:

- A good person learns from a wink, a bad one learns from a kick.
- One who has no good for his family has no good for any other.
- He who loves you, beats you.
- I have neither a she-camel nor a he-camel in this matter. (Meaning: I have no interest in the matter.)
- Throughout its lifetime, the tree never reaches its God. (Meaning: Don't be too ambitious; be content with what God has provided you.)
- He who observes the calamity of other people finds his own calamity is lighter.
- What has been written on the forehead, the eye will see. (Meaning: What has been ordained by God will happen sooner or later.)
- He who does not listen to the older people will fall in the well.
- Where there are no people, there is hell.
- Older than you by a day, wiser than you by a year. (Meaning: Respect older people and their advice.)

Banners in Arabic script in a city center.

THE SCRIPT

Arabic writing goes from right to left and books begin from what the Westerner would call the back. There are no capital letters, but many letters change form depending on their position in a word. There are several different styles of writing, some of which are difficult to read. The ancient style of written Arabic is elaborate and decorative and forms the basis of calligraphy.

The style in newspapers and magazines, called modern standard Arabic, is less elaborate but still difficult for Arabic learners because the marks that indicate vowels with short sounds and twin consonants are not used. Without these marks, the meanings of words can often only be interpreted by context. Imagine reading English with short vowels not printed: "hat," "hit," "hot," and "hut" would all be spelled "ht!"

BODY LANGUAGE

Arab speakers stand very close to each other and use lots of grand and exaggerated gestures—another form of hyperbole. They also speak loudly. Unlike what may be perceived in the West, these characteristics do not represent aggression.

Jordanians use several head movements to communicate with or without speaking. A quick upward movement of the head with raised eyebrows, often accompanied by closed eyelids and a click of the tongue, means "no." A downward nod to one side means "yes."

Arabs gesticulate a lot and can often convey their intentions without actually speaking.

Hand gestures here are similar to those around the Mediterranean basin. The palm turned upward with the fingertips together forming a tent over the palm, the hand and forearm pumping up and down, and the arm flexing at the elbow means "Wait a minute." The palms up and open with arms out to the side and raised as if to lift something means "I don't know," or "I don't understand what's going on here." Open hands drawn quickly above the shoulders, palms facing the other person, means "That's my point!" Finally, the hands rubbed together quickly as if washing means "I'm finished with the matter."

OTHER LANGUAGES

Nearly all educated Jordanians speak some English, and those who are college-educated often speak it quite well. Even most Bedouins speak a little English since many of them depend heavily on tourism for economic support. Only a handful of people speak languages other than Arabic and English.

ARTS

JORDANIAN ART IS mostly tradition-bound in design, materials, and colors. It comes predominantly in the forms of handicrafts such as fabrics, wood, and jewelry, and in language and music.

ANCIENT ART

The Romans and Greeks left their artistic legacy in the land that is now Jordan. The Roman art here is Byzantine and differs noticeably from that of the western Roman empire in Europe. Some Christian art is preserved in churches, monasteries, and convents.

ISLAM'S EFFECT ON ART

Traditional art in the Middle East reflects the role of Islam in daily living. Buildings and utensils were often decorated with religious motifs. The visual arts in all Arab countries adhere to the Islamic ban on human representation, based on the doctrine that only Allah can create life. Instead, there is a proliferation of calligraphy that takes the elaborate shapes of the Arabic alphabet and verses from the Koran and combines them into ornate designs.

Although some predominantly Muslim countries ban all kinds of representational art, Jordan does not. In fact, it encourages and supports a wide variety of art, both traditional and modern. However, most visual arts still focus on geometric and plant designs.

Poetry, often with religious inclinations, was the earliest art form to flourish and was passed on by word of mouth, as most of the people were illiterate.

Above: **A 7th century mosaic in the Church of Apostles in Madaba.**

Opposite: **An artist packs colored sand into bottles to a preconceived design.**

MUSIC

Jordanians respond in the same way to both music and language. This is easy to understand since music and language share certain characteristics in Arab culture. They are repetitive and exaggerated, yet full of subtleties, and rich in stories about honor, family, and love.

Traditional Arabic music is different from Western music. The latter uses half and whole notes with an eight-tone scale, while the former uses quarter notes and a five-tone scale. The music has a special sound and beat and is highly elaborate. It has an intricate rhythm and is fairly ritualized in form. A single musical composition may last for half an hour. The instruments are usually played to accompany vocal music; there is very little purely instrumental Arabic music.

Classical Arabic music uses the oud (an instrument belonging to the lute family), the *kemancha* ("ke-MAHN-cha," a type of violin with a gourd body and only one string), and small lap-held drums. In addition, two types of flute are commonly used in Jordan. One is called *zamr mujwiz* ("ZAH-mr MUJ-wiz"), while another variety used by the Bedouins is called *nay* ("NAY").

Modern Arabic music often uses an orchestra of mostly European instruments, sometimes accompanied by a full choir. Audience participation is encouraged in the form of clapping and cheering. Nowadays, however, Western music is very popular, especially among teenagers, and several Jordanian pop and rock musicians play imitations of it. Others incorporate elements of both modern Western and classical Arabic music with some interesting effects. Indian, Persian, and northeast African music show characteristics that are similar to Arabic music because early Arab traders spread Arab culture during the 8th and 9th centuries. Spanish flamenco music has its origins in Arabic music.

LITERATURE

Jordanian literature is Arabic literature. Poetry—usually oral—has always been the primary form of literary expression in Arab culture, although scholarly or religious works (always florid in style) are usually classified as literature too. Arab poets think strictly in images rather than concepts. By the mid-20th century, strong feelings against foreign domination and Zionism found their way into poetic and literary works.

According to people who study Arabic literature, it can be divided into three main periods: classical, from ancient times to the 16th century; Renaissance, from the 18th century until around the time of World War I; and modern.

Books with a religious theme sold at an outdoor stall.

CLASSICAL Arabic literature was strictly oral for hundreds of years, incorporating the poetry and proverbs of the Bedouins. Many of these were eventually put into writing in the 7th and 8th centuries A.D. After the advent of Islam, all Arabic literature was filled with imagery from the Koran.

The earliest form of written poetry was called *qasidah* ("kah-SEE-duh"), meaning "purpose poem." These poems had between 20 and 100 verses and were usually an account of a journey. There would be a love poem prologue, followed by a long narrative of the journey, then an epilogue that flattered the host and heaped scorn upon his enemies. For centuries Arab poetry followed this formula until it eventually became too pompous and exceptionally verbose, even for the Arabs themselves, and died out.

Another form of classical poetry, called *ghazal* ("GAH-zl"), followed the prologue (love poem) form of the *qasidah* but was used for religious and other subjects as well. These were five to 12 verses long. A form of verse known as *qit'ah* ("KIT-uh") was less serious and used for jokes and word play.

Prose, although not nearly as popular or prevalent as poetry, took the form of simple true stories told in an exceedingly complicated and wordy manner, full of word play, double entendre, and complex imagery. These were called *maqamah* ("mah-KAH-mah"). Classical Arabic included no epic fiction of any kind.

RENAISSANCE Ironically, the revival of the nearly defunct Arabic literary tradition began after Napoleon Bonaparte conquered Egypt in the 18th century. Writers from all over the Arab world flocked to Cairo for its freedom of expression and came into contact for the first time with European literature. Although the literature of this renaissance was built upon foundations of classical Arabic literature, it began to incorporate elements of European literature. It became introspective and nationalistic. The most common form of writing in this time was the historical novel.

MODERN In the late 19th century, when European Jews began to move into Palestine (of which Jordan was still a part), Palestinians began to see the problems that such an influx would cause and began to write about it. This trickle became a flood after the creation of the state of Israel in 1948, after which most Palestinians became virtually homeless—both for daily shelter and a land to call their own.

Great literature is often born of tumult and disaster, and the displacement of hundreds of thousands of Palestinians was the flash point of modern Arabic literature. Surprisingly, however, the literature of the Palestinians did not simply become political and polemic; writers strove to show the moral bankruptcy and stagnancy of Arab culture in general. Many wonderful women writers wrote about the real situation of women in the Arab world. Other writers felt it important to record the daily life of the people, and a culture that had been nearly lost with Jewish control of Palestine.

The latter attempt became stronger after the 1967 war, when the West Bank and Gaza Strip were occupied by the Israeli military. From then until Israel and the Palestine Liberation Organization signed their first agreement on the road to Palestinian self-rule, Palestinians who remained in the two conquered territories had no citizenship, no passports, no constitutional rights, and were allowed to do only what the Israeli military authorities allowed them to do. They were people in limbo.

Palestinian poetry of the late 20th century was described by one scholar as portraying with subtlety and esthetic sophistication a genuinely existential situation, told in infinitely rich terms. Despite the predominant use and importance of poetry, Palestinian literature also uses the short story and novel to great effect. Modern adaptations of Western literary models are gaining acceptance as well.

"... when a truthful woman speaks, it is life that is speaking."

—*Fadwa Tuqan, Palestinian poet*

THE WORDS OF THE POETS

Here are words of some Jordanian-Palestinian writers that paint pictures of their situation.

Mona Sa'udi: "I find myself rootless and abandoned like a stone. Without love, there is no meaning to life nor to art. Why can't a man love a woman without having to choke her, to shut her up, controling her mind, her dreams ... how can we love in freedom, not in oppression, only the woman is capable of that!"

Fadwa Tuqan (in response to her father's demand that she write more "political" poetry): "How and with what right or logic does father ask me to compose political poetry, when I am shut up inside these walls? I don't sit with men, I don't listen to their heated discussions, nor do I participate in the turmoil of life outside. I'm still not even acquainted with the face of my own country as I was not allowed to travel."

Fadwa Tuqan (in *Enough for Me*):
Enough for me to die on her earth
be buried in her
to melt and vanish in her soil
then sprout forth as a flower
played with by a child from my country.
Enough for me to remain
in my country's embrace
to be in her close as a handful of dust
a sprig of grass
a flower.

Samira Azzam, from the short story, *Bread of Sacrifice*:
That spring, Ramiz learned about two things—love and war—and the first gave meaning to the second. War was not simply an enemy to kill voraciously. Rather, it was the assertion of the life of the land he loved and the woman he loved. Palestine was not only a sea with fishing boats, and oranges shining like gold, and not just olives and olive oil filling the big oil jars. It was Su'ad's black eyes as well. In Su'ad's eyes he saw all of Palestine's goodness.

Poem by Ghassan Zaqtan (*A Mirror*):
Two faces loom in the catastrophe
my father and his horses; a little moon
that we will capture sails above our house.
If only we could regain our childhood,
we'd imprison that moon
a while between our hands,
and when our hearts
opened, let it fly away.

Literature and various forms of written expression are regarded as noble forms of creative pursuit.

WRITERS

Some of the best-known and most-respected writers of Jordanian origin are Fadwa Tuqan, Samira Azzam, and Mona Sa'udi (all women); poets Ibrahim Abu Naab, Gassan Kanafani, and Mustafa Wahbah at-Tal; and fiction writer Mahmoud Sayf ad-Din al-Irani. Al-Irani, who died in 1974, lived in Amman from 1942 and worked as a teacher and school inspector. He was a pioneer of the short story in Arabic literature, and his writing illustrates the inseparability of Jordanian and Palestinian cultures.

Today, for the first time in Arab history, there is some experimentation with writing literature in dialect rather than standard Arabic, but this is

"As happens in backward societies where a woman's life revolves around trivialities ... the family environment offered me nothing; rather, it only increased my burden.

—Fadwa Tuqan

AN ANCIENT BEDOUIN FOLK TALE

In the search for new grazing pastures, a Bedouin tribe sent out a raven, a partridge, and a dove to look for grass. The raven returned quickly saying there was no grass to be found. The partridge and dove came back later saying that there was grass "soft as a lady's hair" within two days' journey.

The Bedouins traveled to where the partridge and dove had seen the grass, and found it. To punish the raven, they colored it black to represent deceit. To reward the dove, they applied henna (a traditional Arab ochre dye) on its feet, just as they would a young Arab bride. To reward the partridge, they decorated its eyes with black lines of kohl (a dark-colored dye used as eyeliner).

not widely accepted. In fact, conservative Muslims feel it is almost a heresy as they believe the Arabic of the Koran to be God's own words and language. The sentiment is that it is all right to speak differently, but written language must conform to standard Arabic.

HANDICRAFTS

Jordanian handicrafts reflect two main influences: Bedouin and Palestinian.

Large, heavy gold necklaces, bracelets, anklets, earrings, and rings in elaborate designs are one way in which wealth can be invested and displayed at the same time.

GOLD AND SILVER Bedouins have been creating elaborate jewelry for centuries, and this tradition shows in modern jewelry. Middle- and upper-class Jordanian women wear a lot of striking gold and gold-toned jewelry, including large earrings and lots of bracelets, some with extremely fine filigree designs. Bedouin and village women, on the other hand, do not usually wear gold, but silver. Bedouin and village women who wear scarves and veils often decorate them with chains and other adornments. Necklaces with charms and large hoop earrings are widely worn. Most jewelry sold in Jordanian souks and shops, as with other handicrafts, are made by the shopkeepers themselves.

WOODWORK Another typical Jordanian handicraft is wooden mosaics of two basic types. One uses thin layers of factory-made veneers; the other has each piece of wood, bone, or mother-of-pearl cut and set by hand. Creating the latter is slow, painstaking work. The most common products are various sizes and shapes of boxes, trays, tables, and game boards. Jordanian artisans also carve objects from olive wood.

Woven handicrafts for sale. From childhood, daughters watch their mothers working at the looms and soon learn the art of creating the elaborate designs and vivid colors.

FABRICS Carpets and clothing (especially gowns and robes) are the main fabric arts in Jordan. These days, most carpets are made for sale to tourists. Weaving is done by women using a hand loom and wool dyed in bright colors.

Bedouin women and rural Palestinians still make traditional jackets, skirts, and various types of gowns for men and women. These are decorated with much embroidery. Palestinian embroidery is highly valued for its intricate, colorful designs that take months or years to create. The embroidery is used on jackets, the fronts of skirts, gowns, and pillows.

USE OF RUGS

Nomads travel light for practical reasons. The ideal way to make a tent that is comfortable yet light is to use fabric. The typical Bedouin tent (and often, village house) has carpets that cover the entire ground, and these are piled with large cushions on which the family sits and sleeps. The fabrics are woven from sheep, goat, and camel wool on horizontal, hand-built looms. Large carpets cover the floors, while smaller ones are used as prayer rugs.

Each prayer rug has the geometric shape of an arrowhead at one end, and this is placed pointing toward Mecca when praying. These little carpets make a comfortable praying site, no matter where the believer might be, when the call to prayer is heard.

Desert sand to take home. Colorful sand patterns packed into glass bottles are popular with tourists.

BOTTLED SAND One craft unique to Jordan is the art of packing multicolored sand into small glass jars, forming designs that range from geometrics to plants and animals, and scenes of the desert. Minute funnels are used to put small amounts of the sand into desired spots, and the design takes shape from the bottom of the container upward. The sand is continuously tamped down firmly, to keep the design from crumbling. Once the jar is full and the artist is satisfied, the sand is tamped firmly and the jar opening plugged with plaster.

GLASS BLOWING This is a minor craft in Jordan, mostly to make tea glasses (Arabs do not drink tea from cups), small dishes, and water pipes called *argheeleh* ("ahr-GHEE-lay") in Arabic and "hubble-bubble" by most foreign visitors.

MODERN ARTS

Amman has numerous art galleries, and there is a significant number of painters and sculptors in Jordan. Jordanian art reflects strong influences from American and European art of this century, but also embodies elements of Arab culture. Some Jordanian artists are quite expressive, and their themes include love, the struggle for a Palestinian homeland, environmental destruction, and overpopulation. Unfortunately, Arab culture does not generally respect the visual arts beyond its decorative value, and most artists in Jordan struggle for economic and social survival to an even greater degree than those in the United States or Europe.

"HUBBLE-BUBBLE" WATER PIPES

Each *argheeleh* ranges from about 10 inches (25 cm) to 3 feet (90 cm) in height, usually has a hand-blown glass body and brass fittings, and stands on the floor. Sweet tobacco that has been cured with honey or sugared water is placed on the small tray on top of the *argheeleh*. A red-hot piece of charcoal is placed on top of the tobacco. At the bottom of the *argheeleh* is a water trap through which the smoke is sucked through a long, woven hose.

Sucking the smoke causes a pleasant bubbling sound that gives rise to its nickname of "hubble-bubble." The smoke smells sweet and feels cool in the mouth. Many Arab men (and also the more "liberated" women) smoke the *argheeleh* after evening meals, especially when eating out in restaurants.

ARCHITECTURE

Islamic architecture features high ceilings, small windows, and thick walls. These help to keep the interior of the building cool, even in hot weather. Traditional buildings face inward, overlooking an internal courtyard that often has a fountain. Domes and arches add a distinctive touch.

LEISURE

AS WITH ALL ARABS, rich or poor, urban or rural, socializing is the main source of entertainment and consumes a large part of every person's spare time. Generally, Jordanians do not have hobbies as many Americans or Europeans do. Many of them do not enjoy reading, tinkering with mechanical things, building things, boating, or engaging in sports.

DINING

Meals with friends and family, at home or in a restaurant, are often major social events. Lunch is the preferred time for socializing as it is often the biggest meal of the day. Two to three hours can be spent socializing, eating, and drinking tea. Long dinners are common among affluent city dwellers.

Above: **Time for a family meal. Meat dishes are a favorite.**

Opposite: **Jordanian men enjoy their leisure relaxing and chatting with friends.**

Fridays, the official "weekend" in Jordan, are favorite days to spend outdoors. After attending prayer sessions in the mosque, many Jordanians spend the entire day eating, talking, strolling the streets, or traveling short distances to restaurants outside town.

Dressing in their best clothes is important and socializing is the main occasion for which to dress up. Even conservative Muslim women often wear fashionable scarves and dresses. Young people scout for a potential marriage partner—even if their efforts remain only a dream.

Unlike citizens of neighboring Syria and Lebanon, Jordanians do not mill around the streets on warm evenings. Amman's streets are quiet by 10 p.m. or 11 p.m., when most people are at home or in restaurants.

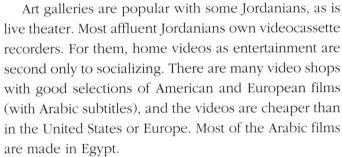

Opposite: **Traders take a coffee break. The coffee is thick, has a strong flavor, and is taken without milk.**

Below: **Men in working clothes pause for a rest in the noonday heat.**

OTHER ACTIVITIES

Art galleries and concerts are found mainly in Amman. Wealthy, Westernized Jordanians attend concerts in droves, and their musical exuberance is usually obvious, even at classical music concerts. Arab people relate so strongly to music that most simply cannot sit still while a catchy tune is playing.

Art galleries are popular with some Jordanians, as is live theater. Most affluent Jordanians own videocassette recorders. For them, home videos as entertainment are second only to socializing. There are many video shops with good selections of American and European films (with Arabic subtitles), and the videos are cheaper than in the United States or Europe. Most of the Arabic films are made in Egypt.

Magazines and newspapers from the United States, Europe, and all Arab countries are available and uncensored in Jordan. Such press freedom is highly unusual in an Arab country and keeps literate Jordanians more in touch with the outside world than most other Arabs. Glossy picture magazines are also popular.

Trips to the beach or outings to public parks are very much a family affair. Women often gather with other women for limited social activities or just to talk.

Guests are often received at home with a display of great hospitality. Foreign visitors are made to feel very welcome. Jordanians are happy to act as hosts and guides and keen to inform others about their culture and traditions.

FAVORITE PASTIMES

All Muslim societies are sexually segregated. Whole families may socialize together, or else the men join other men while women and children join other women and children. A few public activities are taboo for women. These include standing on the streets talking to friends, eating in restaurants without the presence of a male family member, going to a tea or coffee house, and smoking in public. Men, on the other hand, spend most of their free time doing these things with other men.

Older men, in particular, make a fine art of whiling away their time. They sit in tea houses drinking tea or Arabic coffee (a concentrated mixture served in small cups). Other pastimes are smoking the *argheeleh,* talking, or playing board games. One such game is the mancala, one of the world's oldest and most widely played games. Even shopkeepers spend a great deal of time indulging in the various pastimes when customers are scarce. On Thursday nights young men often hang out with male friends, talking, going to exceedingly violent movies, or just watching passing young women, who are almost always with their families.

While men hang out in the streets, tea shops, and cinemas, women are usually at home working hard, shopping for the family's needs, or chatting with daughters, sisters, mothers, and neighbors.

SPORTS

In an Arab country such as Jordan, the idea of competitive sport is relatively new, although camel and horse races have been held by Bedouins for centuries. The sport has gone professional, with races held on tracks outside the main cities in the late afternoon. Islam forbids gambling, but that does not reduce the excitement of a race.

As a spectator sport, soccer is the favorite of modern Jordanians, although the country has no official team. If a World Cup match is on, the men will be glued to their television sets no matter who is playing. Generally only young, wealthy Jordanians play any kind of organized sports once out of high school. The major cities have a few tennis courts and running tracks but no golf courses. There are several diving centers along the coast of Aqaba. However, the sport is popular among tourists only, as the Arabs generally do not take to sea sports.

Traditional, wealthy men practice the ancient Arab sport of falconry that involves hunting with falcons, a type of hawk. A few men still hunt in the desert, but since so much of Jordan's wildlife is endangered and thus off limits, hunting is not a serious sport.

Top: **Waterskiing in Aqaba.**

Above: **Only the wealthy indulge in the sport of falconry. For them, fine falcons are prized possessions.**

106

CINEMA, RADIO, AND TELEVISION

Cinemas show English-language movies as well as Middle-Eastern staples. Since 1989 an annual European film festival has been held in Amman around May. Foreign cultural centers have regular film screenings as well.

There is a great variety of both radio and television programs. Radio stations play current and classical Arab music, some English-language programs, classical European music, and Western hits. The British Broadcasting Corporation's World Service can also be received. Radios are often played outdoors during warm weather, with the volume turned on high.

There are several Jordanian television stations, a few from

Cinema posters in Amman.

Lebanon, and one or more—depending on geographic location—from Israel. Jordanian television broadcasts mainly in Arabic, but also in English. French programs are broadcast from Lebanon, and Hebrew programs from Israel. The Jordanians are avid television watchers and follow American soap operas, soccer, and wrestling programs.

FESTIVALS

JORDANIAN SOCIETY DOES NOT OBSERVE MANY festivals since celebrations are included in everyday socializing, births, weddings, and religious traditions. Of all these, weddings are celebrated most extravagantly.

WEDDINGS

These are celebrated in different ways depending on whether the family is Christian or Muslim. They reflect the overriding importance of the family in Arab culture and are often planned and executed with complete abandon.

In traditional Muslim families, males celebrate separately from females before the wedding ceremony. When a family does not have a lot of money (particularly in rural areas), the men celebrate in the streets, and the women at home. The men clap, chant, and dance to the sound of a drum, while the women talk, laugh, and belly dance for each other. After the ceremony there will be feasting, talking, and dancing—again, usually segregated by gender—that may last for several days.

Less traditional Muslims as well as Christians with lots of money may rent a hotel ballroom and eat, drink, and dance all night, usually with the men and women celebrating together.

Above: **Modern couples often choose to marry in Western-style clothes.**

Opposite: **Members of the Royal Jordanian Armed Forces Band provide a rousing touch to national events.**

RELIGIOUS FESTIVALS

These are the second biggest festivals after marriage parties, and the Muslim festivals are both the longest-lasting and the liveliest.

MUSLIM FESTIVALS Although not a festival per se, Ramadan—the ninth month of the Islamic calendar during which devout Muslims fast from sunrise to sunset—includes feasting in an evening meal called *iftar* ("IF-tar"). It also includes special mosque services every evening and a great deal of socializing and public activity after dark. For *iftar* special foods are prepared that are eaten only during Ramadan, large quantities of food are served, and the extended family is present. During the last few days of Ramadan, clothing stores stay open especially late so that people can buy the new clothes they will wear during the three-day holiday called *Eid* ("ID") that follows the end of Ramadan. To an observer, Ramadan evenings have all the attributes of a festival.

Eid is observed twice. The first comes immediately after Ramadan; the second, after the *hajj*, or pilgrimage. During these festivals people eat special foods (especially sweets) and stay up all night socializing with extended family members and friends. Carnival rides are set up in city and village parks, horses and donkeys are rented for children to ride in the streets, and everyone wears new clothes. The first *Eid* seems more like a festival than the second. Perhaps this is because most Muslims fast, but only a small number make the *hajj* in any one year. During both *Eid* festivals few businesses or shops are open, government offices and schools are closed, and many people go away to resort areas.

The dates for *Eid* are determined by the Muslim calendar and the first one also by the visibility of the moon. Even though they are officially celebrated over three days, it is common for some businesses, schools, and embassies to close for a whole week.

CHRISTIAN CELEBRATIONS Christmas is celebrated by all Christians, Eastern Easter is celebrated by Eastern Orthodox Christians, and Western Easter is celebrated by Roman Catholics and Protestants. The two Easters usually fall one week apart. Because of the small number of Christians, the celebrations are low-key and there is little festivity in the streets. Government offices, schools, and Christian businesses are closed for the holidays.

One will not find Christmas caroling, Easter egg hunts, decorated streets, or Christmas trees in public, but some businesses are beginning to decorate their stores in order to cash in on the festivities. The stores are also generally busier, catering to those who need to get gifts for loved ones and friends.

Christmas and Easter holidays are celebrated in the homes of believers in much the same way they are in the West, with special meals, gift-giving, new clothing, and Christmas trees and decorations. The churches hold special masses or other services, and there is much rejoicing.

Portrait of a three-handed Virgin Mary in a church in Madaba.

Camel and horse races appeal to locals as well as foreigners. Tourists who miss the events may get to ride a horse or camel while visiting the desert ruins of Petra instead.

OTHER CELEBRATIONS

Jordanians celebrate, with special music and dancing, events such as births, circumcisions, funerals, plowing, planting, and harvesting. These are governed by tradition and the entire family takes part in the rituals.

TOURIST ATTRACTIONS In order to generate some much-desired tourist income for the country, Jordan sponsors and publicizes several events. One is the camel and horse festival, which includes camel and horse races, and special talent and breed shows.

There are two major festivals every year. The Jerash Festival for Culture and Arts takes place every August over a two-week period and includes daily performances by Jordanian, Arab, and international folk troupes and performers. The Aqaba Sports Festival in mid-November includes world-class competition in water-skiing and other aquatic sports. Then there is the hot-air balloon festival in Wadi Rum. Concerts are held occasionally in Amman's Roman theater.

DANCING FOR LIFE

Few of the traditional dances performed in Jordan are organized presentations for which people buy tickets and sit and watch. They are performed by ordinary people in the same costumes and with the same movements that have been in existence for many generations. The most common forms of rhythmic accompaniment for dancing are pounding feet, clapping hands, and small drums. One dance, the *debkah* ("deb-KAH"), is Jordan's most popular. It bears similarities to Spanish flamenco, which started with dances brought to Spain by Arab conquerors 1,200 years ago.

The Bedouins have their own dance called the *sahjeh* ("SAH-jeh"), illustrating grand stories of heroic deeds. The Circassians have a special sword dance, accompanied by music, and there is a special troupe that performs for the public. The troupe has appeared on television and traveled abroad to perform, and its music is sometimes played on Jordanian radio stations.

Top and above: **Traditional dance costumes for men and women.**

FOOD

JORDANIAN FOOD IS SIMILAR to that of its neighbors Syria, Lebanon, and Iraq. Lamb is consumed in large quantities and yogurt, chicken, bulgur, parsley, eggplant, garlic, tomatoes, rice, and flat bread constitute the bulk of the average person's diet. Seasoning is mostly accomplished with garlic and mint. Dates are also important when in season and are used in some traditional sweets. Some of the basic recipes originated from the Ottoman Turks during their long occupation of the area.

MEALS

Breakfast is usually eaten quite early, especially in Muslim families, because the men get up at dawn to pray, and eat afterwards. School children also start the day early, around 6 a.m. in the summer. This means that the mother and older sisters must get up early to prepare the food. The largest meal of the day is generally lunch, which is served around 2 p.m. Dinner is light (except during Ramadan, special feasts, or when eating out) and is always eaten after 8 p.m. Coffee or tea follows every meal, whether eaten at home or in a restaurant.

MAKING BREAD

Arabic bread is made from wheat flour. Bedouin women and poorer families make the flour themselves using traditional grinding stones. Usually, enough is ground for each day's needs. The wealthier families buy flat bread from the bakeries. A common sight in villages and cities is people walking home with large stacks of bread every morning. Many women carry the bread on their heads. To make the bread, the flour is mixed with water and a little salt, but no yeast. There is a variety of tastes and textures, depending on how the bread is baked. At home, baking bread is a woman's task. The bread is round and flat and eaten with all types of food. It is usually used to scoop up various dips, cheese, or meat.

Tucking into Bedouin *mansif,* prepared from lamb.

TYPES OF FOOD

Jordanian food is hearty fare with lots of meat—mostly lamb and chicken—and heavy dips that are scooped up and eaten with flat bread. Perhaps the most ubiquitous food item in Jordan is the olive, which is eaten with every meal as well as for snacks. Olives are available in dozens of varieties, ranging from enormous to tiny, from yellow to black, from bitter and dry to sweet and juicy, and from crunchy to soft. Olive oil, clarified butterfat called ghee, and lard rendered from the tail of fat-tailed sheep are used extensively in or on nearly all food.

MAIN COURSES Breakfast is always light, and usually consists of cheese, olives, and bread—sometimes with jam. For lunch, the big meal of the day at home, a favorite—and maybe the most common dish—is an old Bedouin concoction called *mansif* ("MAHN-seef"). This is made from lamb, yogurt, and rice and simmered for a long time. The Bedouins still eat it the traditional way—scooped up with bread or the fingers, but some modern Jordanians use a fork. Various other dishes with lamb, vegetables, rice, and lemon are also common. Marinated and barbecued chicken, called *shishtou* ("shish-TA-oo"), is popular, especially among city people.

116

Certain foods are made in large quantities and bottled to last for a year or more. One of these is *maqtub* ("MUK-toob"), made of small eggplants stuffed with spiced meat and then pickled. Small zucchini-type squash is also cored and stuffed with a rice-meat mixture for a dish called *kusa meshi* ("KOO-sa MEH-she"), which is prepared in advance.

In restaurants that serve Arab cuisine (all of which have basically the same menu), lamb kebabs, *shishtou*, and breaded and fried lamb medallions are the most common entree.

THE TRIMMINGS   Before the main course is served at home, *hors d'oeuvres* such as shish kebabs, small, spicy meatballs, cheese, pickles, and olives might typically be served. Along with the main course people often eat soup—usually either lamb-broth, vegetable, or lentil—and a salad called *fatoush* ("fah-TOOSH") that includes mint and bits of yesterday's flat bread fried crisp in oil. In restaurants that serve Arab cuisine, *hors d'oeuvres* consist of various creamed dishes made from eggplant, chickpeas (also called garbanzo beans), and yogurt. The dips are eaten by scooping them up with bits of fresh flat bread. Salads are also popular, especially one made with yogurt, cucumber, mint, and garlic.

Eating out is convenient and a wide range of local favorites is available.

Favorite drinks are canned carbonated beverages, tea, coffee, and *laban* ("LAY-bun")—a yogurt, water, and garlic drink. *Laban* is the Arabic word for yogurt. All meals, whether at home or in traditional Arab restaurants, are accompanied by trays of olives, raw vegetables such as peppers and carrots, pickles, and sometimes cheese made from goat's or sheep's milk.

SWEETS AND SNACKS Although Western-style treats such as ice-cream and pudding have become popular among affluent people, the dense, traditional Arab confections are still very popular. These are delicious, but rich and sweet. They include a lot of nuts (especially pistachios), coconut, and spun sugar. Equally popular for dessert are trays of fruit such as melons, bananas, grapes, peaches, and plums.

INTERNATIONAL FOODS Jordanians, having been exposed to the West in various ways for several generations, have developed a taste for nontraditional foods. Aqaba has a Chinese restaurant as well as several seafood restaurants that serve European-style menus. Amman has numerous Italian and Chinese eating

Above: **Kebabs being prepared. Slices of spicy, minced lamb are pressed onto skewers and grilled over a charcoal fire.**

Opposite: **Bedouin drivers stop by an Arab cafe in Amman.**

establishments. The luxury hotels throughout Jordan serve a large variety of cuisines, and breakfast buffets that include Arab, American, and European foods are popular.

ARAB FAST FOOD

There are no international fast-food chains in Jordan, but there is a local version of fast food. Small shops and street vendors make something like a sandwich (but which is more like a burrito), which they call *shawarma*. It consists of thinly sliced lamb or chicken rolled up with garnishes and sauce in a small piece of flat bread. Other shops sell *falafel* ("fah-LAW-fel") sandwiches—crumbled *falafel* (deep-fried croquette of ground chickpeas or fava beans, and spices) mixed with yogurt, parsley, and other foodstuffs, and also rolled up in flat bread. Chicken shops sell whole roasted birds stuffed with rice or cracked-wheat mixtures, as well as fried chicken and French fries.

Also, depending on the season, decorated carts on street corners sell unripened almonds (a sour treat one dips in salt before eating), boiled corn-on-the-cob, roasted chestnuts, fresh pistachios, unripened plums, and various other treats.

IN A JORDANIAN KITCHEN

Middle- and upper-class Jordanians equip their kitchens in a style similar to European or American kitchens. They often have appliances such as dish washers, food processors, and microwave ovens. The poorer people, and those who are more traditional, use only basic utensils that require much muscle power and human energy. They buy large quantities of food items such as eggplant and core it to make their stuffed eggplant dishes. They do similar, extended operations with other vegetables. This work is always done by the women, and it is a lucky mother who has one or two daughters to help with the chores. In traditional homes men do nothing to help prepare food.

CHILLED CUCUMBER *LABAN* SALAD

4 cups yogurt
4–6 cloves garlic
4 medium-sized cucumbers

1 teaspoon salt
1 tablespoon dried mint leaves or
¼ cup fresh, chopped mint leaves

Stir the yogurt until creamy.

Peel and mince or crush the garlic, then blend with the yogurt.

Peel and chop or slice the cucumbers thinly, then add to the mixture.

Add salt and most of the mint.

Serve in a bowl with the remaining mint leaves sprinkled on top (rub the dried mint leaves between the palms and let the bits fall over the salad).

DAILY SHOPPING

An Arab woman's work never ends. In addition to cooking most of the day and taking care of numerous children, a husband, and sometimes older relatives, she usually does the family shopping. Jordan's only supermarket is located in Amman. It is open 24 hours a day and provides Amman residents with the chance to buy turkeys from the United States, asparagus from France, and various other goods that are not available in Arab souks. Most other shops in Jordan are small by Western standards and usually sell a narrow range of foods. Grocery stores sell canned goods and packaged goods. Fruit and vegetable stands sell local and some imported produce, and butchers often have only chicken or lamb.

There are four types of bakeries: one for the traditional Arab flat bread, one for French-type baguettes, one for elaborately decorated European-style sweets, and one for traditional Arab confections. Since most groceries are bought fresh every day, shopping requires a great deal of time. In some conservative Muslim families, the fathers and sons do all the shopping to avoid having their women on the streets dealing with other men.

Vegetable stall in a souk. The vegetables are usually prepared with other foods or pickled.

121

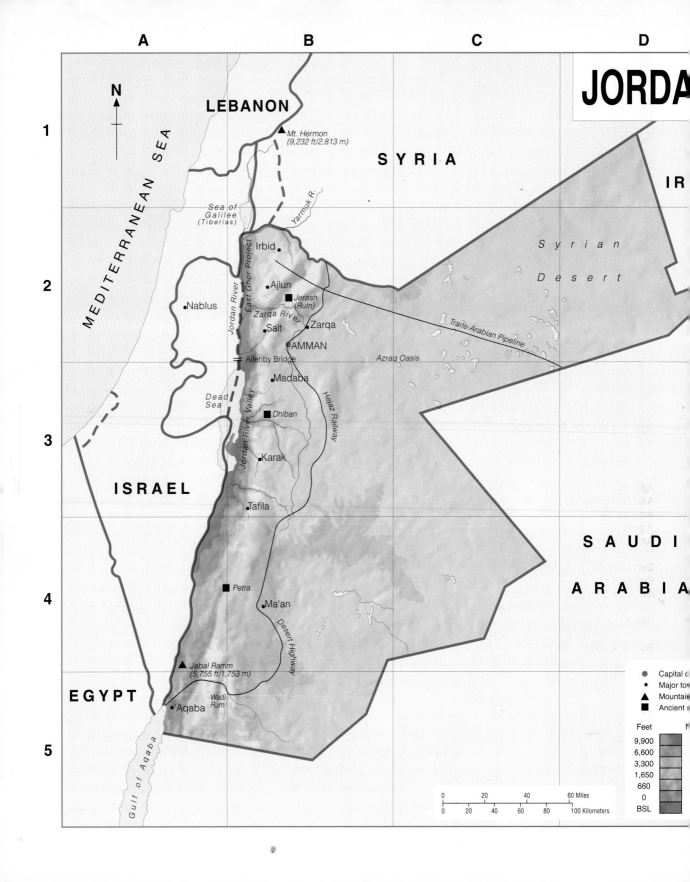

JORDA

A   B   C   D

N

LEBANON

SYRIA

IR

1

MEDITERRANEAN SEA

▲ *Mt. Hermon*
(9,232 ft/2,813 m)

Yarmuk R.

*Sea of
Galilee
(Tiberias)*

Syrian

Desert

Irbid

East Ghor Project

Ajlun

2

■ *Jerash
(Ruin)*

Zarqa River

Zarqa

Jordan River

•Nablus

Salt

●AMMAN

Trans-Arabian Pipeline

Azraq Oasis

Allenby Bridge

Madaba

Hejaz Railway

*Dead
Sea*

Jordan River Valley

■ *Dhiban*

3

Karak

ISRAEL

Tafila

SAUDI

ARABIA

■ Petra

4

Ma'an

Desert Highway

▲ *Jabal Ramm
(5,755 ft/1,753 m)*

EGYPT

•Aqaba

*Wadi
Rum*

Gulf of Aqaba

● Capital c

• Major tow

▲ Mountai

■ Ancient s

Feet   N

9,900
6,600
3,300
1,650
660
0
BSL

5

| 0 | 20 | 40 | 60 Miles |
| 0 | 20 | 40 | 60 | 80 | 100 Kilometers |

QUICK NOTES

OFFICIAL NAME
The Hashemite Kingdom of Jordan

AREA
35,000 square miles (90,700 square kilometers)

POPULATION
4.3 million

OFFICIAL LANGUAGE
Arabic

TYPE OF GOVERNMENT
Constitutional monarchy

TERRITORIAL DISTRICTS
Amman, Irbid, Ma'an, Al Mafraq, Al Karnak

CAPITAL
Amman

MAJOR CITIES
Zarqa, Irbid

GEOGRAPHICAL REGIONS
Jordan River Valley, plateau and highlands, desert land

RIVERS
Jordan, Yarmuk, Zarqa

OTHER BODIES OF WATER
The Dead Sea, Gulf of Aqaba, Azraq Oasis

HIGHEST POINT
Jabal (Mount) Ramm; 5,755 feet (1,753 meters)

LOWEST POINT
The Dead Sea, 1,300 feet (396 meters) below sea level.

NATIONAL FLAG
This consists of a black stripe on top, a green stripe at the bottom, and a white stripe in the middle. The left end bears a red triangle with its point in the center of the white stripe. In the center of the triangle is a seven-pointed white star representing the first seven verses of the Koran.

NATIONAL ANTHEM
Long Live the King!

OFFICIAL RELIGION
Islam

MAJOR RELIGIONS
Islam, Christianity

CURRENCY
Jordanian dinar; divided into 1,000 fils
US$1 = 0.75 dinar

MAIN EXPORTS
Chemicals, phosphates, and manufactured machinery

GLOSSARY

al Hamdullah ("ahl HAHM-dool-lah")
Phrase meaning "Thank Allah."

argheeleh ("ahr-GHEE-lay")
"Hubble-bubble" water pipes for smoking.

Badoo ("BAH-doo")
"Desert dweller," the Arabic name for the Bedouins.

corral
Enclosure for cattle or horses.

Eid ("ID")
Three-day religious celebration and holiday following the fasting month of Ramadan. Also the holiday following the Muslim pilgrimage to Mecca.

fatoush (fah-TOOSH")
Salad with mint and flat bread fried crisp in oil.

Hejaz ("hee-JAZZ")
Provincial area of western Saudi Arabia, along the Red Sea and Gulf of Aqaba, formerly an independent kingdom. In 1932, it united with the sultanate of Nejd to form Saudi Arabia.

insha'allah ("in-SHAH-ahl-LAH")
A phrase commonly quoted that means "God willing," when talking about the future.

Kaaba ("KAH-AH-bah")
Building covered with black cloth standing in the courtyard of the Great Mosque in Mecca.

kaffiyeh ("kah-FEE-yay")
Traditional Arab headdress for men.

laban ("LAY-bun")
Yogurt, water, and garlic drink. Also refers to plain yogurt.

Levant
Former name for the lands on the eastern Mediterranean shore now occupied by Lebanon, Syria, and Israel.

maha ("MAH-hah")
Oryx. Literally "crystal."

mansif ("MAHN-seef")
Meal made of lamb, yogurt, and rice simmered for a long time and eaten with bread or scooped up with the fingers.

maqtub ("MUK-toob")
Eggplant stuffed with spiced meat and pickled.

raka ("RAH-kah")
Prayer ritual.

Shari'a ("shah-REE-ah")
Islamic law.

Sunna ("SOON-nah")
Teachings and examples set by Prophet Mohammed.

wadi ("WAH-dee")
Canyon.

Zionism
Political movement for the establishment and support of a national homeland for the Jews in Palestine, now concerned chiefly with the development of the modern state of Israel.

BIBLIOGRAPHY

Bakalla, M.H. *Arabic Culture Through Its Language and Literature.* London: Kegan Paul International, 1984.

Civilizations of the Middle East. Milwaukee: Raintree Publishers, 1989.

Gumley, Frances. *The Pillars of Islam: An Introduction to the Islamic Faith.* London: BBC Books, 1990.

Helms, S.W. *Jawa: Lost City of the Black Desert.* New York: Cornell University Press, 1981.

Jordan in Pictures. Minneapolis: Lerner Publications, 1988.

Khadra, Salma (Ed). *Anthology of Modern Palestinian Literature.* New York: Columbia University Press, 1992.

Matusky, Gregory & Hayes, John P. *King Hussein.* New York: Chelsea House Publishers, 1987.

Nevins, Edward & Wright, Theon. *World Without Time: The Bedouin.* New York: The John Day Company, 1969.

Shami, Seteney, et al. *Women in Arab Society.* Oxford: Berg Publishers Ltd, 1990.

Tuqan, Fadwa. *A Mountainous Journey: An Autobiography.* Translated by Olive Kenny and Noami Shihab Nye. St Paul, Minnesota: Graywolf Press, 1990.

INDEX

INDEX

INDEX